T0386762

THE LIBYAN PARADOX

The CERI Series in Comparative Politics and International Studies

Series editor CHRISTOPHE JAFFRELOT

This series consists of translations of noteworthy manuscripts and publications in the social sciences emanating from the foremost French research centre in international studies, the Paris-based Centre d'Etudes et de Recherches Internationales (CERI), part of Sciences Po and associated with the CNRS (Centre National de la Recherche Scientifique).

The focus of the series is the transformation of politics and society by transnational and domestic factors—globalisation, migration and the postbipolar balance of power on the one hand, and ethnicity and religion on the other. States are more permeable to external influence than ever before and this phenomenon is accelerating processes of social and political change the world over. In seeking to understand and interpret these transformations, this series gives priority to social trends from below as much as to the interventions of state and non-state actors.

Founded in 1952, CERI has fifty full-time fellows drawn from different disciplines conducting research on comparative political analysis, international relations, regionalism, transnational flows, political sociology, political economy and on individual states.

Luis Martinez

The Libyan Paradox

Translated by John King

HURST & COMPANY, LONDON
*in association with the Centre d'Etudes et de
Recherches Internationales, Paris*

First published in the United Kingdom by
C. Hurst & Co. (Publishers) Ltd,
41 Great Russell Street, London, WC1B 3PL
© Luis Martinez, 2007
All rights reserved.
Printed in India

A catalogue data record for this volume is available
from the British Library.

ISBN–10 1-85065-835-8
ISBN–13 978-1-85065-835-1

CONTENTS

Foreword by Lisa Anderson   *page* vii
Map of Libya   xiv

Introduction   1

   From the business of revolution to a revolution in business   1
   Libya: a model "conversion" of a rogue state?   4
   The price of rehabilitation   8

1. The End of the Embargo   13

   The Jamahiriya: the reckoning   14
   "Halting the wheel that spins in a void"   19
   The dissolution of the government and the establishment
     of the Sha'biyat   22
   The social consequences of sanctions   24
   From Arab unity to racial discrimination   25
   Feelings of isolation and frustration   30
   The economics of plunder   31
   The "young revolutionaries" and the voyage to Malta:
     Rai music, sex, money and sport   35
   The emergence of new economic resources   37
   Conclusion   39

2. 11 September 2001: The "Conversion" of a Regime   43

   The impact of the ivasion of Iraq: fear of inclusion
     in the "axis of evil"   45

v

The effort to resume normal relations with the United States   48
The end of terrorist ambition   52
Joining the coalition in the "Global War on Terrorism"   56
The appearance of Islamist guerillas   60
The Libyan Islamic Fighting Group   61
The LIGFG's strategic deficit   68
The regime's response to armed revolt: repression,
    decentralisation and liberalisation   70
Conclusion   80

3. Gaddafi: His Power and Position   85

The bases of power   88
The maintenance of authority   91
Gaddafi's role: between the revolutionaries and the reformers   104
The United States of Africa   107
Libya and the Euro-Med partnership   111
Conclusion   113

4. Is the Jamahiriya Reformable?   117

Libya: a Metiterranean Eldorado?   119
Libyan blandishments   120
The curse of oil?   124
Necessary but impossible reforms   130
The foreign policy uses of oil income   133
The return of the American oil companies   134
EPSA IV   136
Strengthening relations with Europe   141
The economic costs of Libya's revolutionary policy   144
The end of the Algerian model of development   147
Conclusion   150

Conclusion: After Gaddafi?   153

Notes   159
Index   179

ACKNOWLEDGEMENTS

To my wife Maria and my daughters, Mélissa and Léna

I would like to thank the *Centre d'Etudes et de Recherches Internationales* of the *Fondation Nationale des Sciences Politiques* for its constant support. I am indebted to Lisa Anderson for enabling me to pursue my research at the School of International Public Affairs at Columbia University, New York (2000-2001). I also owe my gratitude to The World Center for the Studies and Researches of the Green Book (Tripoli) for inviting me to take part in its international conferences and meetings. My thanks are also due to the French ambassador to Libya, Jean-Jacques Beaussou, for his hospitality. In Libya, I am deeply grateful to all those who extended their kindness in welcoming me and for their trust in offering to share their opinions. Last, I thank Jamel for helping me to discover and appreciate his beautiful country.

FOREWORD
Lisa Anderson

In May 2006, the United States restored diplomatic relations with Libya after a hiatus of nearly three decades. The move was described by US Secretary of State Condoleezza Rice as having been "in recognition of Libya's continued commitment to its renunciation of terrorism and the excellent cooperation Libya has provided to the United States...in response to common global threats faced by the civilized world since 11 September 2001."[1] Popular interpretations of this somewhat surprising about-face on the part of both the US and Libyan governments focused at the time on the very public and, as Secretary Rice put it, "historic" decision by the Libyan government to renounce terrorism and abandon its weapons of mass destruction program at the height of the American-led Iraq war in 2003. Yet for many observers, the factors which led the United States to reassess its stigmatization of the regime of Mu'ammar al-Qaddafi remained mysterious. After all, the Libyan government's apparent repudiation of terrorism and weapons of mass destruction might have been less than completely sincere—Qaddafi himself suggested a measure of skepticism when he observed during the celebration of his 33rd year in power in 2002 that "we must comply with international legality even though it has been falsified and imposed by the United States, or we will be slaughtered."[2] Moreover, what exactly was the nature of Libya's "excellent cooperation" in sharing intelligence about regional terrorist groups and why should Libyan-supplied information be trusted?

If the American rationale for embracing the Qaddafi regime was murky, the Libyan motives in "coming in from the cold" seemed to be almost completely opaque. The decade-long United Nations sanctions regime between 1992 and 2003 had obscured life in a country that many observers had already found baffling by making it almost completely inaccessible to foreign visitors, including researchers. What accounted for the apparent change of heart in one of the world's most fervent anti-imperialist revolutionaries?

Luis Martinez is one of the very few international scholars who can venture informed answers to these questions. He has followed domestic Libyan politics closely for more than two decades, throughout the American embargo and during the United Nations sanctions, and he brings an intimate familiarity with the country to his analysis. He has seen first hand the domestic impact of half a century of oil revenues, nearly four decades of permanent revolution, twenty-five years of American hostility and more than a decade of international isolation, and he is eloquent in describing what this poisonous combination has created.

It is a shadowy world of illegal weapons, ideological zealotry, terrorism, wealth and waste, hypocrisy, frustration, corruption and family intrigue, occasionally leavened by flashes of genuine patriotism, generosity and foresight. How much of this toxic mix can be attributed to "the curse of oil," to the upheavals that attended constant revolution, to the impact of inaccessibility and chronic shortages? Martinez refuses to apportion responsibility but he does demonstrate that while the sanctions may have been a boon for the regime at the outset, serving to distract popular attention from dropping oil prices and bureaucratic mismanagement, they eventually contributed to growing corruption—both petty smuggling and more serious fraud, currency speculation and money laundering by senior officials. The resulting popular dismay and disappointment, in turn, fed domestic opposition.

By the mid-1990s, an armed Islamist opposition had appeared, composed at least in part of Libyan veterans of the war in Afghanistan. Suddenly, as Martinez deftly illustrates, Libya's regime was more of a *status quo* government than the "opposition-on-a-global-scale" that Qaddafi had styled himself. Although its isolation limited international media attention to the conflict, the country was wracked by armed battles, assassination attempts and declarations of martial law. Soon Libya looked more like neighboring Algeria, then in the throes of civil war, than the bastion of revolutionary rectitude it claimed to be.

By 1998, when Libya issued the first Interpol warning about the threat posed by Usama Bin Laden and al-Qa'ida, the Qaddafi regime had clearly calculated the growing costs of international isolation. The government would eventually estimate that the sanctions had cost Libya upwards of 30 billion dollars, and that did not include foregoing the military and security cooperation with the West that the Algerian regime, for example, had enjoyed in its own battle with its armed Islamist opposition.

It was in that context that a new reformist faction emerged on the Libyan political scene, led and exemplified by Saif al-Islam al-Qaddafi, Mu'ammar al-Qaddafi's third-born son. As the US's then Assistant Secretary for Near Eastern Affairs Martin Indyk would later write, "Libya's representatives were ready to put everything on the table, saying that Mr. Qaddafi had realized... that Libya and the US faced a common threat from Islamic fundamentalism."[3] As it happened, it took nearly a decade and the events of September 11, 2001 to bring the American and Libyan governments to terms—and, as Martinez shows, the lifting of the sanctions would to be only the beginning of the road to recovery for Libya.

In June 2003, a reform-minded Prime Minister, Shukhri Ghanem, was appointed and his government pushed domestic reform very hard and very fast: retail trade soon flourished, international banks set up branches, Libyans resumed traveling abroad in large numbers, the American oil companies returned in force, there was talk of developing tourism. For some Libyans this was a welcome relief from decades of international isolation and Qaddafi-style socialism. For others, including both those who had profited from the corruption that developed under the embargo as well as those who simply knew little beyond the now-thirty-seven-year regime of Mu'ammar Qaddafi, not all the changes were welcome. Western-style capitalism clearly appealed to some Libyans while repelling others, including those who worried that, in promoting freedom, the regime would abandon its historic commitment to equality. In March 2006, shortly before the diplomatic fruits of his labors were finally to be fully realized, Ghanem was removed as Prime Minister.

As Martinez suggests, although the international sanctions under which the country labored for so long had been lifted, the work of defining the nature of the new regime in Libya had just begun. Qaddafi was deeply disappointed with the failure of the Libyan people, not to say the rest of the world, to embrace his vision and only reluctantly acceded to the restructuring advocated by his son, Saif, and his reformist colleagues. Most Libyans in turn were deeply skeptical about the intentions of any of the government factions— reformers and old guard alike. No visitor could fail to notice the ever-present trash strewn along streets and highways throughout the country, a trivial but telling indication of the mutual disappointment of the government and governed. Certainly most Libyans were ready for change but there was a deep weariness mixed with the wary optimism greeting its arrival. As Martinez so eloquently shows, this was a people exhausted by revolution, deeply dismayed by their current circumstances, angry about the corruption that sustained nearly everyone during the sanctions era, but equally deeply distrustful of upheaval.

There is no doubt that one of the first steps along the path to repairing this deeply wounded country will be to understand the challenges it faces. On that score, Martinez has provided a great service not only to the European and American scholars and policymakers who will now once again turn their attention to Libya, but to the Libyan people themselves.

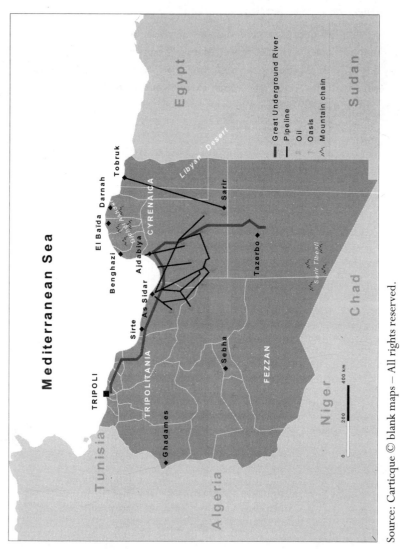

Designed by Dorian Ryser, CERI, using Cartes&Données™ software.

Mediterranean Sea

Egypt

Sudan

Chad

Niger

Algeria

Tunisia

TRIPOLI

TRIPOLITANIA

Ghadames

Sirte

As Sidar

Ajdabiya

Benghazi

El Baïda

Darnah

Tobruk

CYRENAICA

Libyan Desert

Sarir

Tazerbo

Sebha

FEZZAN

Sarir Tibesti

Great Underground River
Pipeline
Oil
Oasis
Mountain chain

0   200   400 km

INTRODUCTION

From the business of revolution to a revolution in business

This book displays how a revolutionary State — historically anti-imperialist, anti-colonialist and anti-Zionist — has "converted" itself into an adherent of the "New World Order", as defined by the Bush administration in the aftermath of the terrorist attacks of 11 September 2001 in New York. It provides an analysis of the mechanisms through which this change took place. The era of the United Nations sanctions, from 1992 to 2003, was a key stage in the transformation of the Libyan regime. During the course of that decade, the revolutionary institutions of the regime divested themselves of their ideology and became what could truly be described as predators on Libyan society. The disjunction between the Libyan people and the regime was consummated. For the Libyan population, subject to the painful consequences of international sanctions, the extortion practised by the revolutionary institutions sounded the knell for their expectations of the State, whose legitimacy had essentially depended on its ability to redistribute the country's oil income in the form of goods and services.

The revolutionary artifice of the Jamahiriya† crumbled under the impact of the sanctions. The revolution was lost to view, amidst violence and corruption. As to the "authority of the people", this became

1

a shadow of its former self in which the Libyan people could no longer bring themselves to believe. The Jamahiriya became an empty shell, within which were heard the reverberations of power struggles and the cries of predatory entrepreneurs. Economic crisis and tensions in foreign policy prompted the regime to take action. Observation and analysis of such responses yield valuable information on the regime's mechanisms and defences. The sensation of isolation experienced by the people during the sanctions went hand in hand with a profound national disenchantment within Libyan society. The "tribalisation" of the government gave rise to unease over the bases of the national community: was Libya a nation-State, or a State of tribes?

The domination of Libya's oil resources by members of the clans linked to the regime revealed the regime's degeneration into a "mafia", for whom Libya's "black gold" was a powerful instrument of personal enrichment. In reaction to the sanctions, the regime closed ranks, forming tightly-knit inner circles of government. The sanctions revealed that three such centres of power were situated in three separate locations. These were the revolutionary institutions, the National Oil Corporation (NOC) and the Libyan Arab Foreign Investment Company (LAFICO). These three structures — in the fields of security, oil and finance — may be seen as the backbone of the regime. The revolutionary institutions guarantee the security of the regime. The NOC is a crucial part of the regime's machinery, furnishing the Jamahiriya's with its constant flow of funds. The third centre of power is LAFICO. Nicknamed the "cassa forte" (the strong box) by the Italians, it owns assets in a hundred countries and a dozen offshore centres, all administered from its modest offices in central Tripoli.

After the lifting of the international sanctions in September 2003, Libya presented the image of a country committed to the reform of its economy and a reorientation of its foreign policy. What, however, was taking place in the political sphere? And was the regime susceptible to reform? This study shows that one obstacle to major political change was the existence of Libya's oil income. It offers an analysis of the mechanisms by which the regime has sought to entrench its power, and thus raises the question of political change in Libya. Its conclusion is that current changes taking place in Libya, far from conducing to the democratisation of the regime, actually contribute to confirm the regime in what might be called its "authoritarian syndrome".[1]

The basic hypothesis is that a key feature of the Libyan regime is an intermingling of the most intimate kind between the security apparatus and Libya's oil money. This nexus functions as an obstacle to political change.[2] It tends towards the routinisation and frequent employment of violence. It insulates the regime against external pressures. The existence of oil and gas reserves has favoured the establishment of a "mafia" regime, characterised by the domination of the members of a minority social group, by the arbitrary use of violence, and by monopolistic control over the oil income. The analysis of Libya's evolution forms part of the study of the transformation of "rentier States", the power structure of authoritarian regimes,[3] and the project of democratisation in the Arab world.[4]

In this context, a detailed examination of the security apparatus is crucial. The security institutions within what might be called "distributive rentier States"[5] are part of the basic structure of "mafia" regimes. Within the theory of the "rentier State", the State's distributive functions are often seen as more important than coercion. Studies of the rentier State suggest that, by guaranteeing the material well-being of its citizens, the State fends off all kinds of demands that may be made on it. Thus, the distribution of the State's income enables politics to be marginalised and facilitates the purchase of social tranquillity. Consequently, the eventuality of political change is hard to imagine. On the other hand, the examples of Iraq, Algeria and Libya itself largely contradict this hypothesis. Once the early phase of revolutionary fervour is over, such regimes entrench their power principally through coercion. In Libya, during the 1980s and 1990s, the regime made extensive use of violence. Dipping into its deep pockets, the Gaddafi regime built effective security institutions which ensured its survival.

Studies exist that indicate clearly that oil income is a "curse"[6] in the fields of both economics and politics. Is it not accurate to say that the Libyan regime has invested much more heavily in its security than in civil infrastructure? Some of the purposes to which the oil income has been put are military expenditure, the quest for Weapons of Mass Destruction (WMD), the accumulation of capital which has been moved abroad, together with capital projects which were in themselves unproductive but were expedient in terms of foreign policy.[7] In this context, the economic ends for which the oil income has been used demand examination.[8] In Libya, the flood of petrodollars in a State lacking democratic institutions resulted in the growth of corruption. The study of corruption in oil States leads on to a broader issue, namely that of the economic evolution of the rentier State, with the contradiction between the abundance of oil and a level of institutional weakness that calls into question any process of democratisation.[9]

Libya: a model "conversion" of a rogue state?

Rémy Leveau's 1975 study of the social structure of the government under the monarchy of King Idris, from 1951 to 1969, reveals that it depended on a "fragile equilibrium," in which the claims of the urban notables were balanced against those of the tribal chiefs. This equilibrium was destroyed by the discovery of oil and the introduction of a money-based economy. The links of solidarity on which the system of patronage depended were overturned. According to Rémy Leveau, "urban migration, education, and the spread of new ideas emanating from Radio Cairo, all accelerated the process."[10] Libya's revolutionary regime has consolidated its power through the distribution of goods and money, and by means of coercion, but also on the basis of the satisfaction of nationalist ambitions. The imposition of the international sanctions discredited the regime, however, by exposing the predatory activities of some who formed part of it. However, in contrast to the history of the monarchy, the political system did not disintegrate. On the contrary, it was able to exploit and capitalise on the new opportunities afforded by the aftermath of the events of 11 September 2001.

In the course of the 1990s, the Libyan regime was widely seen as being at the limit of its endurance and on the verge of collapse. Its hidden resources, however, must be acknowledged. It overcame the three challenges it faced: the international sanctions; the Islamist guerrilla movements; and a series of coup attempts. For Libya, the attacks of 11 September 2001 came as a stroke of good fortune, and constituted the seminal moment for the Libyan regime's switch of allegiance: its "conversion". To evade the fate of Saddam Hussein's Iraq, Gaddafi's government threw in its lot with the "good guys": the United States and its allies. This switch of allegiance was the choice of a regime whose revolutionary experiment had run its course.

In practice, the "conversion" of the Libyan regime to the "New World Order" ensued from the failure of a political experiment. Libya's far-reaching policy of supporting terrorism, launched in the early 1980s, did not achieve its intended outcome. Libya's colossal expenditure on arms purchases, its research into WMD and the construction of the terrorist infrastructure left it unable to become a military power strong enough to repel a threat within its own territory. After the American bombing of 1986, Colonel Gaddafi said: "If we had possessed a deterrent — missiles that could reach New York — we would have hit it at the same moment. Consequently, we should build this force so that the United States and others will no longer think about an attack. Whether regarding Libya or the Arab homeland, in the coming twenty years this revolution should achieve a unified Arab nation…This should be one homeland, the whole of it, possessing missiles, and even nuclear bombs. Regarding reciprocal treatment, the world has a nuclear bomb, so we should have a nuclear bomb."[11] The regime did not, however, succeed in acquiring such a military deterrent force. The decommissioning of Libya's WMD installations revealed that the regime had been a long way from mastering of the technology necessary to build a nuclear weapon. On top of this inability to copy the Pakistani model came the overthrow of the regime of Saddam Hussein. In order not to bow to the international pressures that were being brought to bear on authoritarian Arab regimes, Libya anticipated the demands of the international community by voluntarily terminating its WMD programme. Libya's "conversion" was part of a range of similar developments which included the future of authoritarian Arab regimes. In this context, Libya sought to become the model of how a "rogue state" could reposition itself,[12] exhorting Syria and Iran to cease their WMD research in order to follow in its footsteps. The downfall of Saddam Hussein's regime was a scenario hitherto unthinkable for the Libyan regime. It led to a line of thought suggesting that the regime was all the more vulnerable since — unlike Pakistan or North Korea — Libya had been unable to provide itself with nuclear weapons.

Until the overthrow of Saddam Hussein, the preoccupation of the Libyan regime had been to maintain in position all the means necessary to bolster its authority. Purges, and the subjection of the army to supervision by the revolutionary organisations, permitted potential coups to be anticipated; the prohibition of political parties forestalled disputes; and arbitrary justice meant opposition could be suppressed without limitation. The survival of Gaddafi's regime demonstrated his mastery of the mechanisms of control available to government. The American-led invasion of Iraq, however, introduced a new factor which caused the regime's authoritarian edifice to tremble. In 1986, the Libyan leadership had responded to the American bombing of Libya with fury and the desire for vengeance. In contrast, the overthrow of Saddam Hussein led to panic and to a new feeling of vulnerability. The apprehension of Libyan officials that the United States might invade Libya became a probability, exacerbating their feeling of insecurity. The rapidity of the Iraqi regime's collapse led the Libyan regime to doubt its own forces and its ability to resist.

The certainty that the regime would be unable to stand up to external pressures brought about internal change. Nonetheless, the process of "conversion" was not artificially imposed: it was rooted in internal demands for change. A new generation of leaders had begun to appear, younger, less formed in their ways by the revolutionary period, and available to lead Libya in the post-sanctions era. The regime had at its disposal an increasing number of new officials in the fields of security and the economy. As this new élite saw it, the post-11 September international system was divided into two blocs: that led by the United States and it allies, and that of the countries which resisted American hegemony. In their view, the key issue was to avoid the "bad guys", Libya's choice in the 1970s when it had aligned itself with the Soviet Union. Henceforth, the way to preserve the regime was seen to be the repositioning of Libya on the "good" side, alongside the United States and its allies. To this end, the regime had two clear advantages. One of these was its expert knowledge of international terrorism, and so far unexploited reserves of oil. To take the lead in this transition, Gaddafi's son Seif el-Islam became the emblematic figure of the new Libya. He was the embodiment of the regime's "conversion" and hoped to see Libya transformed from the third-world revolutionary training camp it had resembled in the 1970s into the Disneyland of the Arab world.

A multitude of conclusions may be drawn from Libya's experience. First, it demonstrates that there is no inevitability about the fate of "terrorist States". With good sense, an abundance of will, and the exercise of imagination, they can evade the tragic fate suffered by the regime of Saddam Hussein. Libya has succeeded in moving from the status of a "terrorist State" to that of a Mediterranean Eldorado with no change in either its leadership or its regime. This display of legerdemain in the field of foreign policy showed the realism of the international community, and in particular of the great powers. Iraq's chaos has left Libya looking, by contrast, all the more attractive. The convergence of Libya's interests with those of the United States, the United Kingdom and France has permitted the dramatic return of Colonel Gaddafi's regime to the international stage. Libyan oil, together with Libya's knowledge of terrorism, have enhanced the appeal of the Libyan regime. The western democracies' feelings of vulnerability in the matter of energy supplies after 11 September 2001 have made an ally out of a former "terrorist State". Only one detail remained to be settled: the cost of Libya's rehabilitation.

The price of rehabilitation

In September 2003, the United Nations Security Council approved the lifting of the United Nations sanctions on Libya. The Libyan government had stood accused of having financed two terrorist attacks. These were the Lockerbie bombing of 21 December 1988, when 259 passengers and eleven people on the ground died after Pan Am flight 103, a Boeing 747, was blown up in the sky over the Scottish town of Lockerbie soon after its departure from London's Heathrow airport for New York. The other incident, on 19 September 1989, was the bombing of UTA flight 772, a DC10, en route from Brazzaville to Paris, in which 170 passengers were killed when the aircraft blew up over the Ténéré desert in Niger. The governments of the United States and the United Kingdom demanded the extradition of two Libyan nationals regarded as the culprits of the Lockerbie attack. The French government asked for the extradition of six Libyan suspects. The Libyan government refused both demands, and on 31 March 1992, in Resolution 748, the Security Council decided to impose the United Nations sanctions on the Libyan government.[13]

In April 1999, after an agreement reached with Kofi Annan, the Secretary-General of the United Nations, Libya agreed to send the two suspects in the Lockerbie incident for trial before an international court convened in the Netherlands.[14] It remained for Libya to resolve its points of disagreement with the Security Council before the sanctions could definitively be lifted. Between the suspension of the sanctions and their final removal, a number of obstacles prevented the resolution of the legal disputes. First, there was the issue of Libya's responsibility. Libya has always refused to accept responsibility for the two attacks, and an early theory identified Iran and Syria as the likely culprits. Under pressure, and as the result of Saudi mediation, Libya finally agreed to the trial of the two Lockerbie suspects. Libya extracted the concession that the trial should not take place in either the United States or in the United Kingdom, as these two countries had demanded, but at the Hague, before an international court. The court's "judgement of Solomon" was the conviction of one of the two suspects and the exoneration of the other.[15] For Libya, the prime consideration was that Gaddafi should not be held responsible, as Head of State, for the terrorist activities of the members of his intelligence services. Once the possibility of any accusation against Colonel Gaddafi had been excluded, and after assurance had been given that no legal steps would be taken against him, the regime opened negotiations on compensation for the families. As the Libyans saw it, the Lockerbie affair had now been brought to a conclusion, and it remained only to settle how much the families were to be paid. The American-led invasion of Iraq speeded up the negotiations, as the Libyan authorities now wished to settle their disputes with the United States at the earliest possible moment.

What then remained was to come to an accommodation with France. Even though the French Examining Judge, Judge Jean-Louis Bruguière, had named the six Libyan suspects, the six men refused to attend the proceedings.[16] In March 1999, they were condemned in absentia to life imprisonment. In April 1999, the Security Council approved the suspension of the sanctions, with France voting in favour. The victims' families were shocked, and expressed their feeling that the French government had abandoned them. The feeling in France was predominantly one of incomprehension: why had the French authorities been unable to exert enough pressure to ensure the presence of the accused at their trial, as had the United States and Great Britain? Certainly, the inclusion of Gaddafi's brother-in-law in the list of suspects made Judge Bruguière's task the more difficult. In fact, the failure by the French authorities to exert pressure was also explicable in terms of France's wish, based on political considerations, to reach an amicable solution between the French and Libyan authorities independently of the demands of the victims' families.

The amount of the financial compensation following the judgement by the Cour d'Assises in Paris was 211 million francs, of which 73 million was reserved for those who had brought civil suits. This resulted in a figure of 35,000 dollars per victim. Unsurprisingly, the Libyan government accepted this figure. For both the French and the Libyan authorities, an end seemed now to have been put to the affair. The suspension of sanctions, and France's expression of good will towards Libya, held out to French businesses the hope of an early return in force to the Libyan market. In the autumn of 2001, the French Minister for Cooperation visited Tripoli in the hope of helping French companies to take advantage of opportunities in Libya. The only fly in the ointment was the continuing indignation of the families of the victims, who found the arrangement reached by France and Libya insulting, and all the more so because French justice had contented itself with the conviction of the accused in absentia.

French public opinion became yet more inflamed when the Lockerbie families obtained a global sum quite out of proportion with that reached under the terms of the Franco-Libyan agreement: 2.7 billion dollars, or 10 million dollars per victim. From then on, the French position changed, and — surprisingly — though France favoured Libya's rehabilitation, France threatened to block the lifting of the UN sanctions if Libya failed to increase its compensation for the families of the victims. For the Libyan side, the affair of the UTA DC10 had appeared closed! The reality was that Anglo-American pressure, against the background of the war in Iraq, had prompted Gaddafi to give generous compensation to the Lockerbie victims. The new international conjuncture had led the Libyan authorities to give temporary precedence to their relations with the United States and Britain. The belated militancy of the French government, together with the threat to obstruct the lifting of the sanctions, irked Libya but nonetheless obliged it to offer an "honourable" level of compensation to the French victims

Two major developments changed the attitude of the Libyan authorities. These were the events of 11 September 2001 in New York, and the United States-led invasion of Iraq launched by the Bush administration. In the wake of these developments, the Libyan government agreed to recognise the "civil responsibility" of the State and declared their readiness to negotiate the level of compensation due to the families of the victims in the UTA incident. In the summer of 2003, direct negotiations got under way between the collective representing the families and the Seif el-Islam Foundation. Libya agreed to give the victims' families one million dollars each. In return, the collective formed by the families committed itself to refrain from any further legal proceedings.

In September 2003, the Security Council voted to lift the sanctions on Libya. Libya then agreed, after negotiations with the United States and Britain, to decommission its programmes for the production of WMD, and to open its nuclear sites to inspection by the International Atomic Energy Authority (IAEA). It also agreed to open up its petroleum industry to foreign participation and expressed its willingness to participate in the "global war against terrorism", as well to free political prisoners and implement other measures. A wind of perestroika appeared to be blowing through the Jamahiriyya. These changes, however, did not presage any real liberalisation of Libya's political system. What took place, rather, was Libya's "conversion". The regime became convinced that its survival depended on the realignment of its economic, diplomatic and security policy to fall in with the priorities of the Bush administration. At the origin of this "conversion" were two seminal moments: the traumatic spectacle of the war in Iraq and the overthrow of Saddam Hussein.

This book describes the evolution of an authoritarian oil regime, faced by unforeseen changes in the international system, and explains how — behind the revolutionary rhetoric of Muammar Gaddafi,

and the liberal approach of Seif el-Islam — there lay similar political practices, characterised by the control and exploitation of the oil
income. Chapter One examines the social transformations which took
place under the sanctions. It shows how, under the sanctions, the discontentment of the population grew, creating fertile ground for the
challenge mounted by the armed Islamists. Chapter Two traces the
unfolding of the regime's "conversion": confronted by armed insurrection within, and the external pressures that followed the events of
11 September, the regime repositioned itself on the "good" side: that
of the United States. Chapter Three looks at the resources on which
Gaddafi's power rests, and offers an account of the secrets of his political survival. Chapter Four shows how a new group has taken control of the machinery of the State. These figures wish to attach Libya
firmly to the western world, employing a strategy of liberalisation
in the oil and gas sector to achieve their goal. Finally the conclusion
shows how thoroughly the regime has accomplished its "conversion".
It now only remains for the regime to prepare for the succession of
Gaddafi by his son.

1

THE END OF THE EMBARGO

International sanctions weakened the regime. Throughout the 1990s, Libya underwent far-reaching social and economic change, which eroded the government's mechanisms of control over Libyan society. In the realm of economics, in the same period, the international sanctions led to the deterioration of Libya's infrastructure, encouraging the growth of an unofficial economy which undermined public confidence in the State's ability to distribute necessary goods and services. In the social sphere, the impoverishment of part of Libya's population provoked rebellious sentiments against a State that seemed to be unable — despite its oil wealth — to assist the most deprived of its people. The sanctions set the scene for criticism of the Jamahiriya and of Colonel Gaddafi's internal and external policies and therefore were in part an explanation for the process of change in Libya. Under the sanctions, the regime was challenged, and Colonel Gaddafi came under attack. Libyan society closed in on itself, allowing the germination of the seeds of a more violent challenge to the regime, in which the immigrant African population became an easy scapegoat.

If the sanctions weakened the regime, they cost the country at large more dearly. In September 1996, the Libyan administration submitted a report to the United Nations Secretary-General Boutros Boutros Ghali, detailing the effects of the sanctions on Libya in the fields of economics, society and healthcare. According to this docu-

13

ment, "All infrastructure development programmes and plans have
been adversely affected, thereby dashing the hopes and aspirations
of the Libyan Arab people to achieve progress, well-being, development, stability, security and peace. Some particulars of the enormous
physical, material and financial damage sustained by the Libyan people during the period indicated above are given hereunder."[1] In the
field of medicine, the Libyan authorities reported that at least 15,570
individuals were in need of personal medical care, and that the sanctions had prevented more than 8500 foreign doctors from coming to
Libya. In terms of the economy, the Libyan document emphasised the
harm done to the transport and communications sectors. Overall, the
government estimated that, by 1998, "the cost of the sanctions has
amounted to 24 billion dollars".[2] The statement by Libyan officials in
2003 that the sanctions had cost Libya more than compensation for
the families of the victims gains credence in the light of these claims.
Following the suspension of the international sanctions in April 1999,
the regime was able to assess the economic and political damage they
had inflicted.

The Jamahiriya: the reckoning

In April 1999, the Libyan population hailed the suspension of the
international sanctions with enthusiasm, seeing in it the end of Libya's isolation. The sanctions had encouraged an unofficial economy
to flourish and had transformed social relationships. Confronted by
Islamic dissidence, the revolutionary regime had tolerated the emergence of an embryonic private enterprise economy in the towns, and
the consequent reappearance of private business in Libya's urban
landscape. In Benghazi, during the sanctions years, the population
grew and urban refurbishment took place. As the years passed, visible
changes occurred. The consumption of alcohol, though it continued
to be banned, was more widely accepted,[3] and the presence of prostitutes fundamentally called into question the regime's puritanical
ethos, though this had rarely been insisted on in practice. In Libya's

impoverished condition, the suspension of the sanctions raised many expectations. For the Libyan people, the economic success of neighbouring Tunisia was a bitter pill to swallow, especially as that country had been regarded in the early 1980s as relatively insignificant when measured against the wealth of Libya. There was a feeling of waste.

The suspension of the sanctions brought with it the observation that in the spheres of both politics and economics the Jamahiriya was in a state of decrepitude. Throughout the 1990s, mounting social tension had signalled the crisis suffered by the population as the result of the collapse in the real value of their incomes. The direct distribution of a proportion of Libya's oil income was intended to mitigate the decline in the living standards of the poorest Libyans. Though the standard of living of the Libyan population was still in many respects higher than that of their North African neighbours, the continued decline in the real value of incomes brought frustrations. During the 1990s, the regime continued to put the blame for its socio-economic problems on the sanctions. In the larger towns, the slogan, "We shall overcome the sanctions," was to be seen everywhere, as if the sanctions were part of some undeserved aggression suffered by Libya. The sanctions actually had the convenient effect of concealing the real causes of the decline of the Libyan economy. In fact, the sanctions even brought profits to certain senior officials within the regime. There was no shortage of public criticism of the money made by certain individuals through currency speculation on the black market, or from the private re-sale of goods subsidised by the State. Though some businesses were closed down, ostensibly as retribution, illicit currency dealing continued with little or no attempt at concealment. Gaddafi, his international position weak due to the sanctions, did not dare make a clean sweep within the Jamahiriya for fear of undermining the very officials who supported him: his closest associates and supporters.

In 2000, the Libyan government launched a 35 billion dollar plan to modernise the country's infrastructure. The international sanctions, together with the collapse in the price of oil during the 1980s had caused a serious economic crisis in Libya.[4] Between 1995 and 1998, grave consequences ensued from the fall in real value of the salaries of the 700,000 State employees amongst Libya's economically active population of 900,000. Post-sanctions Libya had extensive needs, which cried out for foreign investment in every economic sector. Of course, sanctions were not the sole reason for Libya's economic and financial weakness. Extravagant and ill judged economic policies were also responsible for the squandering of resources. Meanwhile, the collapse in the price of oil during the 1980s reduced the government's income from hydrocarbon sales.[5]

Together with the other oil producing countries, Libya was hard hit by the fall in the price of oil after 1985. Libya's income from the sale of hydrocarbon products fell drastically from 20 billion dollars in 1981 to 5 billion in 1986. This loss of income came at a time when Libya was committed to a costly programme of arms purchases. The regime succeeded in compensating for the loss of income, however, principally through its petrodollar investments on the international financial markets. In 1992, for example, the Libyan Arab Foreign Investment Company (LAFICO) managed an investment portfolio estimated at eight billion dollars. Though the Jamahiriya contrived more or less to sustain its war effort in Chad, the standard of living of the Libyan people continued to deteriorate in social and economic terms, whilst the restriction of imports led to shortages that in turn sparked off speculation in foodstuffs. In consequence the regime decided in 1988 to rescind the ban on private commerce, to compensate for the inadequacy of the distribution system. From 1988, Gaddafi initiated a number of reforms linked to the recommendations of the International Monetary Fund (IMF). These included trade liberalisation, the abolition of subsidies on certain products, including grain and tea, together with permission for Libya's agricultural producers to market produce privately. In 1990, a further batch of measures was announced, including the winding up of bankrupt public enterprises, a cut in the number of public employees, laws facilitating foreign investment and the public provision of loans for private businesses. In 1993, schemes for the promotion of tourism and the convertibility of the dinar were set in train. This process of economic liberalisation came to a halt, however, with the United Nations Security Council's decision to impose sanctions on Libya. The priorities of the regime altered, with economic problems taking second place to political and security issues.[6]

Sanctions made the regime more vulnerable. They were also a factor behind the process of change observable in Libya in recent years. The theology of "conversion", which underpins the philosophy of sanctions, had come into play: "In the Wilsonian doctrine, sanctions embody a theology of conversion. The will to reform lies at the heart of the purpose of the imposer of sanctions: the deviant behaviour of the object of the sanctions is to be transformed through punishment."[7] Indirectly, the effect of the sanctions was more to hurt the Libyan people — accustomed to a relatively high standard of living for the region — than to destabilise the Jamahiriya. It has been commented that "the repercussions of the sanctions on Libya's economy and finances were not drastic." On the contrary, "the accumulated increases in consumer prices between 1992 and 1997 amounted to 200 per cent, leading to the deterioration of the standard of living."[8] Despite all this, the sanctions did not reduce the level of oil production, which stayed constant at around 1.5 million barrels a day.

The "punishment" inflicted by the sanctions was more keenly felt by the people. However, it also provoked a significant political crisis between Colonel Gaddafi, as the Guide of the Revolution, and the General People's Congress. After the sanctions were suspended, the scale of Libya's economic difficulties became evident.[10] In January 2000, addressing the General People's Congress, Gaddafi violently attacked the Congress's members: "I must intervene today to halt this wheel which is spinning in a void and is burning oil... You want to stick to your old ways in order to justify the waste of oil.... [Henceforth] this must end! There will be no more sympathy: what we are

	1993	1994	1995	1996	1997	1998	1999
Population (millions)	4.3	4.54	4.7	4.9	5.1	5.3	5.6
GDP (m dollars)	31,716	31,841	32,616	36,419	37,571	34,721	30,851
Oil income (m dollars)	10,025	9.200	7, 605	7,140	7,700	8,010	Not Given
Oil Production mbpd	1.58	1.43	1.36	1.39	1.40	1.40	1.45
Dollar/Dinar (Official rate)	0.28	0.29	0.32	0.36	0.35	0.36	0.39
Inflation (%)	22	17	42	50	30	35	25
GDP per head (dollars: official rate	6700	6500	6000	6500	6500	5800	4900
GDP per head (dollars unofficial rate)	1000	800	700	700	800	800	800

Table showing economic statistics under sanctions[9] (Source IMF, 1999)

talking about here is a revolutionary intervention!" The suspension of sanctions exposed an atrophied economy, totally dependent on oil. The Jamahiriya had based its legitimacy in part on the distribution of its income, and since Gaddafi's seizure of power in 1969, the deep-seated social inequalities inherited by the Jamahiriya had in practice been corrected. In the 1950s, 94 per cent of the population had been illiterate, Libya had no doctors, and infant mortality stood at 40 per cent. In the period from 1951 to 1959, with an annual income of 35 dollars per head, Libya was regarded as one of the world's poorest countries. By terminating the reign of King Idris — who had ruled from 1951 to 1969 — and installing in its place a distributive State, Gaddafi established himself as a genuine benefactor of the people.[11]

During the 1970s and 1980s, Libya underwent irreversible change. The standard of living of the population saw constant growth until it became one of the highest in the region. Libya's growth made it a country of immigration, to which Egyptians, Sudanese and Tunisians came to work. Under the sanctions, this process ended, growth in Libya stagnated, and its funds dried up. In addition, the sanctions disclosed the bankruptcy of Libya's chosen economic system.

"Halting the wheel that spins in a void"

The Jamahiriya survived the ordeal of the sanctions, but not without difficulties. Its development lagged behind expectations. In Gaddafi's words, "Thirty years ago, we took the decision to put 30 per cent of our oil income into covering our operating budget, hoping that each year this percentage would diminish until it reached 10 or 15 per cent, arriving eventually at zero…. But what happened? We have actually reached the point where 100 per cent of the oil income has to go into the operating budget."[12] What had prompted Gaddafi to speak out, he declared, was his "discontent at the waste of oil: the country's sole resource". Libyan society had changed, and social transformations under the sanctions had allowed the population to become aware that the State's disbursement of funds had been selective. The issue of "waste" was increasingly important in a society where youth unemployment was increasingly impossible to ignore. The regime's legitimacy depended in part on its ability to raise living standards. Oil income had led to a passive and unproductive economy — hence Gaddafi's words: "Today, I must intervene to halt the wheel spinning in the void." To this end, Gaddafi announced policies of reform to be followed. First, Libya should "call a halt to fruitless imports," and should instead, "produce and export." Oil income had to be conserved: "Henceforth a red line must be drawn between oil income and other income. Oil should be set aside. Our words, deeds and efforts must be directed towards finding other sources of income. We must build economic sectors which will provide you with income, … suppressing all senseless economic activity…. What I am concerned about today is the welfare of generations to come and the future of the country. A vital issue is at stake. Just as we defended Libya's independence and saved Libya in 1969, it is my duty today to take action to safeguard the country's unique resource." In his pursuit of the "Norwegian model",[13] Gaddafi started from a denunciation of the bankruptcy of the political system. "Were there a proper secretariat of the General People's Congress and officials genuinely selected by the masses, and were there effec-

tive Popular Committees and a General People's Committee, would
it have been left to me to say all this?" Gaddafi then asked rhetorically
whether, "in these circumstances, it is worth making forty years of
sacrifice." Of one thing he was sure: "Those who carried out the revolution were neither scholars nor experts. They were simple revolutionaries. Some among us were unable even to read or write! Others
had failed to graduate from secondary school. We were nothing but
simple unlettered non-commissioned officers."

On the Jamahiriya's shortcomings, he spoke in the following terms
to the General People's Congress: "The present system shall be no
more. When the basic Popular Congresses have been held and following the General People's Congress, what we know as the General
People's Committee shall be no more. Hereafter, there is no "government". The entire system is abolished! Henceforth we shall work
with the "Mahallat" (communes) and the "Sha'biyat" (regional municipalities). You shall no longer be answerable to any higher authority
in Tripoli, Kufra or Sirte, for anything you do within the Sha'biyat:
planning, budgeting and finance.[14] Power will henceforth belong to
the people, the communes and the Sha'biyat." The dissolution of the
government placed local collectivities at the heart of the new political
organisation. In Gaddafi's words: "At the level of the Sha'biyat, you
have everything you need, and secretaries for every sector: health,
education, agriculture, industry. Therefore there is no need to refer
upwards to anyone "in authority". Now you alone must shoulder your
responsibilities. This system will endure for fifty or a hundred years,
until you have grasped it. Only then can we return to the system of
the General People's Committee (i.e., the government)." In the process of completing this "revolutionary intervention", Gaddafi dismissed
fourteen ministers out of the 21 who comprised the government.[15]

This lengthy critique of a system which Gaddafi had himself created
could not fail to arouse questions in the minds of the Libyan people. If
the public sector was ubiquitous, employing 70 per cent of the active
population, this must surely be in part the result of the ban placed

on private business in 1976. As to Gaddafi's allegation that expenses were unchecked, this was the result of there being no mechanism to keep them under control. Actually, it was the context of Gaddafi's "revolutionary intervention" which was significant rather than its content. It was the first augury of impending liberalisation in the existing system, and suggested that the regime could no longer be satisfied with the combination of repressive force with the redistribution of wealth as its philosophy of government.

In the wake of the 1969 coup, the revolutionary regime set up a mechanism, the Basic Popular Committees, whose remit was to rectify the shortcomings of the former monarchist administration, in fields such as business, administration, the media and the universities. By 1973, there were estimated to be 2000 such committees, which constituted the popular base of the new regime. According to the regime's philosophy, the role of the committees was to "participate" in government, which belonged to "the people". However, in 1977, the difficulties experienced in practice by the people in carrying out the duties of government led to the establishment of the "Revolutionary Committees". These were meant to inculcate revolutionary ideas in the people, mobilising them and giving them guidance. The policies of the regime — for example the ban on private business — precipitated the exodus of many leading Libyans in which some 100,000 people left the country as the regime deployed the Revolutionary Committees to carry out the revolution's political aims. Their power reached its peak in the 1980s but began to wane during the sanctions years. In 1998, yet another institution was set up in the shape of the Popular Social Commands. This continual replacement of the popular organisations was accompanied by major administrative reforms intended to coordinate the changes.

Minor modifications were made in the political system in March 1997, March 2000 and again in March 2001. The General People's Congress continued throughout to be the highest body, with five Ministries ("Secretariats") under its control: Foreign Affairs; Economy and Trade; Justice and Security; and African Unity. The others were abolished. The General People's Committee, composed of the Popular Congresses, the regions and the trades unions, controlled the management of public assets, medical services and education, as well as a catalogue of other sectors, including industrialisation, water, transport, agriculture, and publicly owned economic institutions. With the exception of the key Secretariats (Ministries) "the people" were in charge of day-to-day business, but without the power to make policy decisions. At the local level an administrative structure came into existence: the Sha'biyat. Officially these were intended to be a panacea which would resolve Libya's economic and social problems in the post-sanctions era.

The dissolution of the government and the establishment of the Sha'biyat

With bureaucratic inefficiency and growing corruption all around, the new administrative entity (the Sha'biyat), was an element within a plan to increase the efficiency and transparency of Libya's day-to-day political management. The abolition of the majority of the Secretariats — with the exception of the five key Ministries — meant that their powers were transferred to the Sha'biyat.[16] Thirty-one Sha'biyat were established, whose powers in theory embraced the management of local resources, including budgeting and other matters. The Basic Popular Congresses were distributed amongst the 31 Sha'biyat in order to guarantee — in theory at least — that there would be representation for the "people". Each Sha'biya comprised a Popular Committee, its executive authority, together with Secretariats for education, health and other departments.[17] Decentralisation, Libyan style, was a process with roots in history, as Bashir Ghariany points out: "The contemporary experience of decentralization, organization and re-organization took more than 40 years to materialize. It started with three provinces, and after several attempts at restructuring, the country was divided in 2001 into 31 local authorities... "Sha'biyat" is the plural of "Sha'biya", which is the local conglomeration and the cornerstone of the 'popular administration' in achieving the decentralization of authority and performance."[18] The Sha'biyat do their work on the basis of an annual transfer of funds. In practice, "the State determines public services which can be delivered in each different Sha'biya, then undertakes to cover their cost through annual financial transfers."[19] Such economic liberalisation was part of a policy intended to restrain public expenditure whilst encouraging investment and promoting the emergence of local leaderships.

From the political point of view, the process of decentralisation was part of a general move to reassert the central government's control over areas which were escaping from central authority. The influence of the Islamists on small-scale businessmen had attracted the attention of the regime. Throughout the 1970s and 1980s the redistributive State had been the sole provider of goods and services. The exodus of Libya's business class had left the regime as the sole possessor of resources. The resurgence of business activities under the sanctions and the development of an unofficial economy, as well as the demographic explosion, were all threats to the Jamahiriya, which could not stand idly by as an autonomous economy emerged. Clearly, the Sha'biyat were an element in an interventionist policy on the part of the State, which was costly and inefficient in economic terms, but politically and from the standpoint of security remained a necessity. The new administrative structure brought to the fore new leaders, who were obligated to the regime. It also enabled the legitimisation of funds accumulated in the sanctions era by the Revolutionary Committees (by setting up import companies), and provided goods and services to a population which had regarded itself throughout the 1980s as underprivileged. The United Nations sanctions had exposed the bankruptcy of the economic system, and in particular had upset the linkage between Libyan society and the Jamahiriya. In the course of the 1990s, deeper changes began to stir amongst the Libyan population, which called into question the policies of the Gaddafi regime.

The social consequences of sanctions

The changes in Libyan society were related to demography, urban concentration, and the structure of society. In 1973, the population of Libya was estimated at a fraction over 2 million. By 1995, it had reached 5.6 million, of whom 1.7 million were under the age of 15. The increasing youth of the population was a key feature, resulting from a demographic growth rate of 4.21 per cent, one of the highest in the Arab world. In addition to the underlying rate of increase in the population, there was rapid movement of population to the towns.[20] In 1950, the urban population constituted 20 per cent of the total population, but this proportion increased to 45 per cent in 1970, 62 per cent in 1980, 79 per cent in 1990 and 80 per cent in 1995.[21] The international sanctions provoked different reactions from different sections of the population, and most noticeably from different generations. Older Libyans, whose ideas had been shaped by the Revolution, experienced the sanctions as an injustice, while the young saw in them an opportunity for change.

Similarly, the changes in the field of education were substantial. In 1951, Libya had only one university, situated in Benghazi; by 1995, there were thirteen. Student numbers had grown constantly, reaching 269,302 in 1999, as against only 13,418 in 1975.[22] It would be premature to speak of a generational split in Libya. However — as with young Algerians and Moroccans — young people born after the Revolution in Libya have evolved a value system of their own, very different from that advocated by Colonel Gaddafi. They are fascinated by the western model, and have turned their backs on Libya's pan-Arab past. The students make no bones about their disappointment and their expectation of change. That said, criticism of the regime did not begin with the sanctions: as early as 1975, members of the Revolutionary Command Council (RCC) had condemned what they called the regime's revolutionary fantasies. Hervé Bleuchot recalls that one member of the RCC — Omar el-Meshishi — was of the view that "dissent has become widespread." In practice, he said, "the Head of

State can now trust only the members of his tribe, and the officers in the army have been replaced by men from Sirte."[23] Between 1992 and 1999, the population of Libya faced many new problems. The ban on international flights brought a feeling of isolation and marginalisation. The fall in standards of living led to hostile accusations against the regime. The collapse of Libya's currency and the emergence of an unofficial foreign currency market led to unacceptable social inequalities. Feelings of frustration were accompanied by a powerful outburst of xenophobia towards the African immigrants, as well as by jealousy of Tunisia's economic success, and bitterness over the perception of the Jamhirriya's relative failure. Younger Libyans had become weary of Gaddafi, more than half the population not having known any other Head of State. Expressions of dissatisfaction took unexpected forms, and the African immigrants were easy scapegoats.

From Arab unity to racial discrimination

In the spring of 2000, a dramatic turn of events took place which threw into sharp relief the position of the African immigrants in Libya. A hundred or so Africans were "massacred" by what were described as "young Libyans rejecting foreigners in their country".[24] Ali Tikri, the Libyan secretary of the Popular Committee for African Affairs, maintained at a press conference that these murders were not racist: "Racism does not exist among us — we are not white... More than two and a half million Africans live in Libya and only 1700 have identity cards."[25] Such events brought to the fore the bloody contradictions that governed Libya's internal struggle. The sanctions had brought into being a deep-seated sensation of conflict. Violence against African immigrants was, as well as a simple manifestation of racism, a consequence of the impossibility of opposing the regime's policies.

The Jamahiriya — as the "State of the Masses", a revolutionary political system within which each Libyan citizen should be involved through the Popular Committees in political decision making — was affected at the deepest level. By the later 1990s, those who had experienced Libya's original experiment were experiencing a degree of disillusion. For example, one informant, "Tahar", a government employee of ten years standing, who lived in the outskirts of Tripoli in one of the many housing developments built on land donated by the Jamahiriya, had been obliged to become a taxi driver in Tripoli. When interviewed, he was open about his disappointment at Libya's situation, though he did not see it as serious, viewing it rather as paralysed by the political contradictions implicit within the regime:

"'No democracy without popular participation'[26] — it's meaningless; it doesn't work, because you can't mind the government's business as well as your own. Everyone should do his work: if not, things won't go well. We want for nothing: we have olive groves that we leave to rack and ruin, and we all have houses, cars, money. I only work two days a week. Young people lack nothing — their fathers give them everything. When you have a house and a car you don't need much, though food is very dear because of the sanctions and poor people bear the brunt of that because they can't afford to live. But this is because of the political problems — it's only politics." (1996)

Tahar manifests no particular hostility to Gaddafi. Libya's current difficulties cannot — according to him — be blamed on the country's liberator and moderniser. But if Gaddafi himself is not seen as responsible, his political system is seen here as inoperative and, above all, as corrupted by his cronies. Because of Gaddafi's self-proclaimed status as the Guide of the Revolution, he benefits from a general presumption in his favour that absolves him from all responsibility for the Jamahiriya's failures. In addition, Tahar espouses Gaddafi's highly critical views of the merchants and businessmen who profiteer on the back of the Revolution. The part played by the sanctions — and by the same token by the United States — in the deterioration of the standard of living of the Libyan population also serves as an argument for the exoneration of Gaddafi of blame for Libya's present difficulties. For Tahar, Gaddafi remains a charismatic figure and a symbol of modern Libya. He embodies a kind of pride in the face of a world order dominated by the United States, against which his country stands up.[27] Without being a supporter of the Jamahiriya's foreign policy, Tahar nevertheless sees its logic, though he would wish to see it transformed to fit into the regional pattern. All in all, Tahar would like to see its revolutionary ideas reined in, which hurt his country more than they contribute to its development.

In the city of Tripoli, it is clearly amongst those from the province of Sirte that Gaddafi's most fervent supporters are found. However, the Sirteans are also highly critical about the natives of Tripoli and the predilection of the Tripolitanians for making their living from trade and trafficking. Another informant, "Omer", in his fifties, who is employed in a government office but also holds a taxi licence, had lived in Tripoli for fifteen years but did not regard himself as a Tripolitanian, declaring that Sirte, his native town, was the finest in the country. However, he also felt great pride in the capital, with its modern office towers lining the Corniche. In contrast to Tahar, Omer did not accept that Libya's difficulties sprang from the confusion of Jamahiriya policies but believed they came from the presence of immigrants, and from foreign traders who distorted the country's economy:

"We are too generous towards the foreigners and the Arabs.[28] The Libyans don't work and are in the habit of getting all work done by other people. We have allowed lots of Arabs to come here, including Palestinians, Egyptians, Tunisians, Iraqis and even Algerians, and the result is that they are making a lot of trouble for us. The Tunisians and Egyptians do illicit currency deals on the black market, and the Algerians bring in drugs. We are an Arab country, open to the Arabs, but not to all and sundry. It is they who are bringing us down." (1996)

Omer at no time acknowledges that the presence of the non-Libyan Arabs was due to the policy of the Jamahiriya. Nor does he admit that the presence of foreigners was a response to the needs of the Libyan economy, given a Libyan population which was unable achieve by itself the economic objectives of the regime. However, he too echoes Gaddafi's contentions in relation to the problems presented by the foreigners in Libya. The collapse in the real value of incomes in Libya after the drop in the price of oil in 1985, and the speculation in the Libyan dinar which followed the partial economic liberalisation in 1988, had brought resentment against Tunisians and Egyptians accused of profiting from the country's distress. Buses bringing travellers from these two countries encountered barrages of stones and insults from the Libyan population as they passed through Libyan villages. Past hostilities against Tunisia and Egypt were still alive in Libya.[29] In fact, the frontiers with Tunisia had been reopened only as recently as 15 February 1988, not long after the restoration of diplomatic relations in 1987.

The situation of foreigners and non-Libyan Arabs in Libya is revealing both of the Jamahiriya's past policy difficulties and also of present social and political developments, where the non-Libyans present in the country become scapegoats for current problems. In the 1970s, the Jamahiriya had opened its frontiers to the countries of the region, becoming a land of asylum for the revolutionaries of the Third World. Of course, there was an economic motivation for this, namely the need to recruit a workforce,[30] but there were also political considerations. Thanks to the presence of foreigners, the Jamahiriya had at its disposal a reserve of "revolutionaries" able to become members of what was known as the Islamic Legion.[31] However, the successive failures of its external policy — in Tunisia for example, as well as in Chad[32] — spelled out the limited extent to which the immigrants could be made use of. Instead, as oil income fell and speculation drove up the price of food, the immigrants increasingly came to symbolise this miserable period. In Benghazi and Tripoli, the law even turned a blind eye to theft from foreigners. Hashem, a young Pakistani who had worked for five years in Tripoli under the auspices of one of his uncles, described his problems:

"Young Libyans are layabouts who don't want to work. They cheat and steal to make their living. No one stops them thieving from foreigners. Once I caught one in the train in the act of filching my wallet and he just stood in front of me and stared me in the face. I was the one who had to back down, because there is no police force here and the militias are on their side. If you complain, they beat you up. In Pakistan if you catch a thief the police will give him a good beating with their sticks. Here, it's the other way round."

The view that resident foreigners and non-Libyan Arabs were principally responsible for the problems of the Jamahiriya was the reason

for the large-scale and recurrent expulsions of Tunisians, and then
of Sudanese and Algerians. These enabled Gaddafi to go through the
motions of calling a halt to the "scourge", which the presence of immigrants in Libya had supposedly become, while at the same time
keeping a cloak over the true reasons for the difficulties the country
had encountered.

The exhaustion of the Jamahiriya under the sanctions was illustrated by the reluctance of the young to mobilise behind the Guide of the
Revolution. Though those under the age of 20 made up 60 per cent
of Libya's population, the Jamahiriya seemed no longer to be able to
find a place in its machinery for the rising generations. "The State of
the Masses" offered in principle a place for all its citizens to play a part
in making its policies, specifically through the Popular Committees
and the Basic People's Congresses. The Popular Committees were accompanied by the People's Militias, whose task was to keep order. In
practice, however, the political and security structures of the Popular
Committees fell under the control of the Revolutionary Committees[33]
— whose role was to maintain respect for the Jamahiriya — together
with the Jamahiriya Guard, a paramilitary organisation. These were
the sole institutions feared by the population in general as well as the
resident foreigners. The members of the People's Militias were for
the most part young men, unarmed, whose duties consisted of halting
vehicles entering and leaving the towns for the Revolutionary Committees to check the identity of the passengers. Between 1995 and
1998, their sole activity was the erection of crude roadblocks in the
small towns along the coastline from Tripoli to Benghazi. However,
the recruitment of these young men at least meant that there was a
pool of potential future members of the Revolutionary Committees,
so that the replenishment of the supply of guardians for the Jamahiriya
was ensured.[34] The People's Militias could not in any case hope to
arouse fear comparable to that inspired by the Jamahiriya Guard. In
practice, the waning authority of the People's Militias was a factor
in the weakening of the Jamahiriya during the sanctions period. The

Jamahiriya came increasingly to rely solely on the Revolutionary Committees, the Revolutionary Guard, as well as on the Security Services and their networks of informants in the larger towns.

Feelings of isolation and frustration

The embargo on air travel, though frequently breached, was nonetheless experienced as a form of isolation. Of course, this was not the perception of leadership circles, which swiftly devised ways of avoiding it, with the complicity of the air transport authorities in Malta. Ordinary Libyans, however, were able for the most part to leave the country only overland or by sea. In addition to the physical difficulty of making a rapid departure from Libya, the sense of being increasingly placed in quarantine by the international community was what was most keenly felt. The sanctions resulted in a sense of isolation in a country where the erstwhile policy of the regime had been founded on the promotion of a regional Arab order. Bitterness against "brother Arabs" expressed a state of mind reflecting that of the Guide himself.[35] The political outcome was the abolition of the Ministry for Arab Affairs. "Abbas", a student at the University of Benghazi, puts the blame for Libya's problems on its ambition to rectify the injustices prevailing in the Arab world and in Africa:

"The Americans, the Zionists and the French are trying to undermine us because — in contrast to Egypt — we oppose their policies. After the Oslo accords, it was announced that the Palestinians were free to go home, but when the Palestinians in Libya tried to leave, the Egyptians blocked their way and they were stuck at the frontier. The Americans are furious with us because we don't act like Egypt. The French too: they are the ones who are destroying Algeria today — they are taking their revenge! They are doing to the Algerians what the Americans would like to do to us: to crush us. Since the Guide took a stand against France in Chad, and against America, we are alone: just see what this has led to." (1998)

The American policy of the containment of Libya has fostered a feeling of bitterness against such "foreigners" who had hitherto been welcomed as "brothers", though support for this remained diffuse.

On various occasions, Gaddafi has appealed to the Arab League to disregard the sanctions imposed by the United Nations, but in vain.

This sense of isolation has been magnified by Libya's exclusion from the Euro-Mediterranean partnership and by its apprehensions over the new European security policy in the Mediterranean.[36] Similarly, Gaddafi's remarks on the American project for a US-Maghreb trade zone indicate a level of concern over Libya's isolation.[37] Such ideas were perceived as an extension of the sanctions, intended further to undermine Libya. In the event, European and American proposals reinforced the paranoia felt by the Libyan authorities, since they seemed to justify Colonel Gaddafi's strictures against the "New World Order". From this point of view, Libya was being victimised, and the sanctions strengthened the regime. They enabled Gaddafi to distance himself from responsibility for the current problems, and to blame Libya's ills on the international community, which, according to the official rhetoric, was controlled by the Zionists, the authors of Libya's misfortunes.

The economics of plunder

In the small villages of Cyrenaica, it was not uncommon to see fights break out due to shortages in the supply of subsidised bread. The long queues often degenerated into scuffles, after the State bakeries had closed their doors. Those who had failed to get bread would set upon those served earlier, accusing them of taking too much. It was difficult to buy even basic foodstuffs, and "luxury" products, such as cheese or meat, were not to be dreamed of. The existence of this deprivation was all the harder to accept, as it recalled the condition of Libya under the monarchy of King Idris. The intention of Gaddafi's coup in 1969 had been to sweep away the failures of a monarchy accused of contempt for the people's welfare. The deterioration of the standard of living presented a challenge for the Jamahiriya more serious by far than the collapse of its Arab and African policy, raising as it did the spectre of the bankruptcy of the "distributive State". The regime's desire to put the blame for this deterioration on the sanctions was in proportion to the anxiety stirred up by the prevailing social ills.

The regime's response, confronted by this challenge, was to attempt to promote the idea — in the absence of an embargo on oil exports — that the existence of obstacles to oil exportation were nevertheless in some way the reason for Libya's economic problems. It was true that the American sanctions declared in January 1986 and the later United Nations sanctions had brought about a drop in the level of economic activity. In fact, since international sanctions had spared the oil sector,[38] the oil income of the Jamahiriya had been hit, not by the sanctions themselves, but rather by the simultaneous collapse in oil prices. This fall brought with it not only a policy of restriction on imports, but, above all, the renewal in 1988 of permission for Libyans to engage in private commerce, banned since 1973.[39] The intention was to redress the dearth of goods which had resulted from the restriction on imports. Subsequently, many Libyan merchants, who had the resources to make large scale purchases, went to Tunisia, Malta and Egypt to buy goods. In 1988, a million Libyans travelled to Tunisia. From 1995 onwards, however, the value of the Libyan dinar went into steady decline, which prompted the emergence of an unofficial currency exchange market. Tunisian, Maltese and Egyptian goods became unobtainable in Libya, while subsidised Libyan goods were very cheaply bought by traders in neighbouring countries, which were henceforth accused by the Libyan population of stealing the food out of their mouths.

In the sanctions era, a lucrative cross-border trade sprang up. Because of the illicit re-exportation of subsidised Libyan products, Libya was transformed into an "entrepôt state".[40] Under the sanctions, Tunisia became a key destination for Libyans. Between 1988 and 1997, 18.8 million people crossed the border post of Ras Jdir, on Libya's Tunisian frontier.[41] Libyans used the airport at Djerba to travel, and entered Tunisia in large numbers in search of relaxation. With the activities of the tribal groups on both sides, the frontier zone between

Libya and Tunisia also became a conduit for smuggled goods. An un-official market sprang up in the Jeffara plain, run by the Touazine tribe on the Tunisian side and the Nouayel in Libya.[42] The ensuing local prosperity sparked envy and fury in Libya at the spectacle of goods subsidised by the Libyan regime on sale in Tunisia at much increased prices. Nor was the re-exportation of Libyan goods confined to Tunisia and Egypt. Libya, in common with Algeria, became an element in the illicit cross-border network reaching down into sub-Saharan Africa.

Substantial price inflation ensued from the collapse of Libya's currency. (On the black market a Tunisian dinar bought three Libyan dinars instead of one at the official rate, and one Egyptian pound was enough to buy a Libyan dinar). Large profits were made from the re-sale of goods subsidised by the Libyan State on the unofficial market, at uncontrolled prices — to the great irritation of the Libyan public who found nothing for sale in the official marketplace.[43] The principal method of operation of the Libyan businessmen was to sell subsidised products to foreign merchants who made their purchases either in foreign currency or in Libyan dinars bought on the black market. The Libyan vendors thus obtained foreign currency but deprived the Libyan public of subsidised goods. In practice, such illicit re-exportation of Libyan goods could well be described as an economy based on "plunder", and some Libyan leaders made profits from it.[44] According to Emmanuel Grégoire: "Libya floods West Africa with food-stuffs which are cheap because they are subsidised, including Asian rice, pasta, wheat flour, durum flour, oil, soya oil, powdered milk, tomato concentrate, and biscuits. Cheap manufactured goods are also re-exported, including cloth, car spares, electrical goods, light building materials, mattresses, carpets, woollen blankets, and so on. Even four-wheel drive vehicles and trucks are re-sold in Black Africa. A trade in stolen all-terrain vehicles and trucks has begun, with Arab and Tebu traders passing them on into Niger, Mali, Chad and Mauritania.... Finally, a large scale business in trafficking American cigarettes to Libya operates out of Benin and Niger."[45] It still cannot be said, however, that the sanctions were the immediate cause of the deterioration of the standard of life of the Libyan population. What was true, however, was that in the political sphere the Revolutionary Committees, which were a basic pillar of the Jamahiriya, made the largest profits under the sanctions — due to the control they exercised over fraudulent economic activities. The political careers of a number of officials illustrate how a rapid ascent was possible, through the establishment of travel agencies in Malta and Cyprus and by setting up foreign bank accounts in order to feed the Libyan market with consumer goods. The cigarette trade serves an illustration of how the process worked. Emmanuel Grégoire describes the network as follows: "The cartons of cigarettes arrive at the port of Cotonou where they are sent by train to Parakou and by road to Agadès where they are transhipped. The cartons are loaded on to six-wheel trucks which cross the Ténéré desert to Dirkou. There, they are illicitly taken into Libya through the oasis of Tommou, where wealthy merchants from Sebha purchase them, with the connivance of the regional and national authorities. The cigarettes are then distributed throughout the Libyan hinterland.... This is a very large-scale trade amounting to tens of billions of CFA francs each year.... Political figures highly placed within the administration of the Libyan State derive profits from it, since some linked closely to Colonel Gaddafi are involved."[46]

As an institution that operated in the fields of both ideology and security, the Revolutionary Committees were the regime's mainstay during the sanctions period. Though they became the target of vigorous criticism on the part of the Guide of the Revolution toward the end of the 1980s, when he accused them of subverting the nature of the Jamahiriya, they continued to flourish. In a televised speech in May 1988, Gaddafi appealed for them to be condemned by the public. As he put it: "They have lost their way; they have inflicted damage and hurt. A revolutionary should not be an oppressor. I would like to be able to show the contrary to be true: that the Committees love the masses." However, by the end of the 1990s, the 10,000 members of the Revolutionary Committees, together with the 40,000 troops of the Guard of the Jamahiriya, continued to be Gaddafi's power base. They were all from the region of Sirte, and Gaddafi referred to them as the "Ansar" (literally "companions" — the same word used in the expression "Companions of the Prophet"). Together with the business community, they were the principal beneficiaries of the sanctions. Their control over the frontiers enabled them to feed the the unofficial foreign exchange markets.

In reaction to such exploitation of the sanctions on the part of the Libyan establishment, the younger generation of Libyans developed their own network of unofficial trade with Malta. While the sanctions continued, the regime chose to turn a blind eye to these practices rather than halting them. Contrary to widespread belief, the regime no longer depends on terror: the balance between the generations and the play of regional affiliations now articulate relationships between the population and the authorities. In recent years, however, there has been a political split between the younger generation in Libya and the Jamahiriya. This has spread discontent in the furthest reaches of the country, distinguishing the phenomenon from more conventional manifestations of opposition to Colonel Gaddafi's rule.

The "young revolutionaries" and the voyage to Malta:
Rai music, sex, money and sport[47]

With some 60 per cent of Libya's population under the age of 20, the Jamahiriya continues to face the question of how to assimilate the rising generations. Thanks to the still operative redistributive policy of the Jamahiriya, young Libyans are much better off than their Algerian and Moroccan neighbours, but they are not wholly free from financial insecurity. Some young Libyans, especially in Cyrenaica, are in a precarious situation, though not so grave as that of the Algerian younger generation. The connection between the civil disturbances of the 1990s and the process of economic change inside Libya can best be observed in Tripoli itself.

Younger Libyans are fascinated by what they find in Malta. Libyans did not need visas to enter Malta prior to its joining the EU on 1 May 2001 and go there to buy European and American branded goods for resale in Tripoli's unofficial market. The voyage to Malta is also a phase in the sexual education of Libya's young men, thanks to the prevalence there of prostitution. But most particularly it is an episode marked out by the infringement of political taboos. All those who leave Tripoli for Malta will have needed to undergo the ordeal of illegally exporting dinars in order to buy the necessary hard currency on the black market in Valetta. Once this hurdle is overcome, the traffickers revel in the total absence of restrictions on board ship, where virtually all the passengers are young Libyan males. They gather in groups of half a dozen, pool their money and start on the business of making lists of what they intend to buy, and the profits they aim to realise on their return to Libya.

The voyage to Malta provides an opportunity to gain an insight into certain aspects of the political outlook of these younger Libyans. They express their opinions uninhibitedly. The topic of money looms largest in their conversations, unsurprisingly for a group whose central preoccupation is trade. They know that any profits they may make will not amount to much in comparison with the Jamahiriya's big operators. In any case, as they explain, such men will not be making the journey by sea, as — despite the ban on air travel — they have access to aircraft for the journey between Tripoli and Malta. The trade with Malta enables young Libyan traders to stock their shops with the latest fashions, but they are always apprehensive that on their return to Tripoli they may not be able to hold on to their profits, because of the rackets run by customs.

In practice, the route of commerce chosen by the Libyan younger generation signals the limitations of the Jamahiriya's distributive policy. By opening the door to the accumulation of wealth, Gaddafi

hoped to deflect the dissatisfaction of his citizens with a political system that had run out of energy. Such a policy was not immune from
risks. It alienated the 700,000 government officials, loyal servants of
the Jamahiriya, who saw it as a contradiction of the social policy the
Guide of the Revolution had himself laid down. They take a jaundiced
view of the rapid acquirement of wealth by young Libyans who have
succeeded — thanks to a handful of sea voyages — in achieving a
standard of living higher than their own. Their bitterness is felt all
the more acutely, moreover, as this situation has come about with
the acquiescence of the Revolutionary Committees, whose members
nevertheless purport to be the Revolution's guardians. "Hamid", a
friend of Tahar, was an employee in a bank in Tripoli: as he saw it the
"businessmen" (in Libyan Arabic: "biznessa") had more foreign currency than there was in his bank:

"They are very wealthy, the young guys who go to Malta. They never invest their
money; they are always buying things to sell; they recycle the smallest profit.
When they can't make the trip themselves they give their money to friends who
do the buying on their behalf. But it is thanks to them that you can get everything
in Tripoli, except that to buy what they have to sell you have to have plenty of
money!" (1998)

At a time when Libyan civil servants had a monthly income of 250
dinars, frozen from ten years earlier, they saw businesses being set
up that overflowed with the latest goods, at prices they could never
hope to afford.

The emergence of new economic resources

According to Dirk Vandewalle, before the economic liberalisation
of 1988, more than 75 per cent of employees in Libya worked for
the State, where, officially, employees were regarded as partners.
With trade partially freed from restrictions, some members of the
younger generation in Libya saw in the informal business sector an
opportunity for economic autonomy. This breached the principles of
the Jamahiriya by espousing a philosophy of individualism prohibited
by the Guide of the Revolution on the grounds that, contrary to the

egalitarian principles of the Jamahirrya, it re-erected the values of social advancement and hierarchy. One route to attain success was now
based on the voyage to Malta, rather than on the various basic political
mechanisms of the Jamahiriya. Politically speaking, the journey was
a ritual where the full range of possibilities in terms of civil disobedi-
ence and political challenge found expression. As one voyager put it,

"Here [on board the ship] no-one is bossing you about. You can speak your mind
to anybody. There are no policemen — if there were, you'd throw them in
the sea. We all know each other; there is nothing to fear. I make the trip every
month. There are people from Tripoli, and from other places as well. Thanks to
Malta, we all make a good living out of trade."

This process of economic enfranchisement has presented a real challenge to the Jamahiriya. Turning a blind eye to the process calls into
question the principle of egalitarianism; but to bring it to a halt would
run the risk of provoking civil unrest, with incalculable consequences.
It must be said that the administration of the Jamahiriya lost no time
before erecting barriers to any real economic liberalisation. Any such
development would have upset the networks of patronage that under-
lay the Jamahiriya's existence. Such networks existed in the military
field, in the upper echelons of the public enterprises, in the oil industry and in the Revolutionary Committees. However, the non-applica-
tion of economic reform, did not mean a return to the ban on private
trade. Nevertheless, from 1996, private business was subjected to the
scrutiny of so-called "Purification Committees", made up of junior
officers, set up to stamp out private business. In July 1996, a law
defining the scope of "Purification" prescribed the death penalty for
"all those who carry out currency exchange in violation of the regulations of the Central Bank or who export the national currency", and
for those who practise "speculation in foodstuffs, clothes, housing or
transport". More than 1500 businesses were closed down in that year
alone. However, the emergence of the black market, in which up to
20 per cent of currency transactions were carried out at a rate up to
ten times higher than the official rate, had already helped to entrench a

prosperous unofficial economy. The motivation for economic reform was the deterioration of the living standards of ordinary Libyans.

Thanks to the social and economic importance of the unofficial trade to young Libyans, it has continued to be tolerated up to a point. It is true that its effects have gone far beyond the basic trade in consumer goods. It feeds the unofficial currency markets and provides customs agents with a substantial unofficial income. The apprehension of the "biznessa" was always that their holdings in dinars in excess of the permitted sums would be confiscated:

"They say it's our fault that goods are too expensive. They say we bring too much in, and that's why they take our money. It isn't true; they want to keep our money for themselves. In each group, they pick out one trader and take his money. That's how they make their living. Goods are dear because we buy at high prices: foreign exchange costs a lot on the black market. But they buy the same goods with dollars at the official rate, and then they sell them on privately or to foreigners for hard currency. It's because of them that the cost of living is so high." (1998)

Unofficial trade, in fact, has taken on the role of a life raft. It compensates for the difficulties the Jamahiriya has in fulfilling its distributive role. Their percentage guarantees civil servants a decent standard of living, and profits from the resale of goods provide a lucrative and rewarding business for the young Libyan traders. However, unofficial trade raises certain issues, particularly in relation to the principles laid down by Gaddafi in the Green Book. Trade facilitates the social advancement of particular individuals at the expense of the community, and thus poses a threat to the Jamahiriya's egalitarian foundations.

Conclusion

Under the sanctions, the political situation in the Jamahiriya became steadily worse. The regime attempted, with some success, to promote the idea that the sanctions were the principal cause of the deterioration of the country's social and economic conditions. In practice, the effect of the sanctions was to concentrate economic and financial power in the hands of the Revolutionary Committees and of the Jamahiriya Guard, thus ensuring that these played a key role in the process of social redistribution. The sanctions prompted an explosion in the unofficial market in Libya, whose effects on the social changes under way represented a real challenge for the Jamahiriya. After the suspension of the sanctions, the involvement of the younger generation of Libyans in unofficial trade freed them from the constraints imposed by the distributive State, as it was no longer necessary to participate in the Popular Committees or in the Militias in order to have an income. The unofficial markets in hard currency and consumer goods enabled them to take sufficient profit. Despite the ideological anathematisation of private business by the Guide of the Revolution, and the establishment of the Purification Committees, business, both official and unofficial, had the strength to resist the Jamahiriya. This resistance was indicative of social trends, and suggests that revolutionary sentiment had been converted into a movement driven by such values as individualism. Significantly, the popular songs favoured by the young speak of drunkenness, love, easy money and travel.

The revolutionary regime no longer possesses the attributes of legitimacy. It is under challenge from disgruntled Libyans of the younger generation who no longer see the Jamahiriya as a political mechanism able to build a "just society". One dramatic development in particular has symbolically exposed the collapse of the regime's claim to purity — the contaminated blood affair. In 1997 and 1998, during the sanctions period, more than 400 children treated at the paediatric hospital in Benghazi became infected with HIV, and 43 of them died. The scandal has rocked the Libyan public and transformed their perception of the regime. In 2001, Colonel Gaddafi raised the spectre of a plot involving the CIA and Mossad. Five Bulgarian nurses and a Palestinian doctor were arrested and accused of "injecting Libyan children with blood contaminated by the AIDS virus."[48] The Libyan authorities refused to accept that standards of hygiene could have been inadequate, and initiated no search for the source of the contaminated blood, preferring instead the theory of a foreign conspiracy. However, the fact was that, under the sanctions, the number of AIDS/HIV victims had soared, officially reaching an overall total of 1852.[49] By the end of the 1990s, the affair of the contamination of the blood of the children of Benghazi had become a metaphor for the ills of Libyan society. The sanctions were responsible for the deterioration of the infrastructure of the health system, as well as the fall in Libya's productivity and for the weakening of the bonds that linked the Revolutionary regime with Libyan society. Meanwhile the "Purification Committees" were unable to halt the speculative activities of the young traders, to stop the growth of prostitution, or to arrest the decline of the Jamahiriya.

It was within this morally tainted context that the Islamists — who, according to Gaddafi, themselves constituted an infection within society comparable to AIDS — initiated their Jihad against the regime. They launched the first violent attacks against the regime inside Libya itself that had occurred since the coup of 1969. Together with the armed Islamist operations there was civil unrest amongst the younger generation. Up to that time, opponents of the regime had been banished to Egypt or to Chad, and had found their support in regional politics. However, recent years have seen the emergence of the new phenomenon of armed action and civil dissent on Libya's home territory. The Islamist challenge was a response to the supposed decadence of the Jamahiriya. Gaddafi's "just society" has sunk into corruption and debauchery. As the Islamists saw the situation, the time had come to "purify" Libya, as they saw it, from the "sickness" personified, in their view, by its Guide.

11 SEPTEMBER 2001:
THE "CONVERSION" OF THE REGIME

The sanctions have also left the Libyan regime vulnerable. Oil income is no longer sufficient to buy social stability. Libyan society has been transformed, and awaits changes in political direction. A wind of dissent is beginning to rise in Libya. For the first time since coming to power, Colonel Gaddafi has confronted an armed opposition group within Libya: the Libyan Islamic Fighting Group (LIFG) (Al-Jama'a al-Islamiya al-Muqatila bi-Libya). Fragile after the sanctions, and challenged by the Islamist guerrillas, the Libyan regime has grasped the historic opportunity presented by the events of 11 September 2001. Its response to this defining development was to situate itself on the "good" side — that is to say, on the side of the United States.

In his State of the Union speech on 20 September 2001, President George W. Bush of the United States proclaimed: "Every nation, in every region, now has a decision to make. Either you are with us, or you are with the terrorists." Libya, on the US list of "state sponsors of international terrorism",[1] took the unique occasion of the 11 September attacks to reveal its "conversion" to the New World Order. On 16 September 2001, Colonel Gaddafi, in his capacity as Libya's Head of State, declared that the United States has the right to take reprisals against terrorist attacks. Gaddafi's statement came as a surprise. However, it was fully consistent with Libya's ambition once and for all to quit the catalogue of America's enemies. For the Libyan regime, the "terrorist" policies of the 1970s and 1980s were at an end, and the quest for the re-establishment of diplomatic relations with the United States had become a key objective.

On 15 May, 2006, the goal was achieved: the United States announced the re-establishment of "full and complete" diplomatic relations, crossing Libya off the list of states that support terrorism. In the words of Secretary of State Condoleezza Rice's announcement: "We are taking these actions in recognition of Libya's continued commitment to its renunciation of terrorism and the excellent cooperation Libya has provided to the United States and other members of the international community in response to common global threats faced by the civilized world since September 11, 2001."

Since the suspension of the sanctions in April 1999, Libya had undertaken numerous adjustments of its internal and external policies, directed at the re-establishment of Libya's position in the international community and at the permanent lifting of the sanctions. There were signals that Gaddafi wished to be seen in a new light by the international community. Indications of change within the regime included the abandonment of Libya's pan-Arabism, the re-invention of Gaddafi as an elder statesman in Africa, and Libya's political will to reconstruct its relationship with the United States. In addition to these new foreign policy directions, significant social and economic changes made clear the need for a more extensive liberalisation of the Libyan Jamahiriya.

Between April 1999 and September 2003, Libya finally submitted to the demands of the Security Council by agreeing to recognise its "civil responsibility" in the bombing of Pan Am Flight 103. In addition, Libya agreed, after negotiations with the United States and Britain, to dismantle its WMD programme and to open its nuclear sites to inspection by the International Atomic Energy Agency. Three factors explained why Libya speeded up its progress towards normalisation. First, the decline in internal social and economic conditions under the sanctions had left the Libyan leadership aware that the continuation of the sanctions would further undermine the regime. In view of this, the costs of lifting the sanctions would be less than the price to be paid if they were maintained. Secondly, Gaddafi feared that in the aftermath of the US-led invasion of Iraq, Libya would be included in the Bush administration's list of countries defined as the "axis of evil". Finally, Gaddafi's wish to reinstate Libya within the international community appeared to be a preparatory step towards the hand-over to a successor.

The impact of the invasion of Iraq: fear of inclusion in the "axis of evil"

The US-led invasion of Iraq was the catalyst for change. The Bush administration, faced by widespread criticism, pointed to Libya's reaction as an example of the benefits to be obtained from taking a firm political line. The Libyan authorities were quick to perceive the advantages of offering the United States the dismantling of Libya's WMD programme in exchange for the normalisation of relations.[2] Libya had been subjected to unilateral American sanctions since 1986, and the United States had viewed Gaddafi as an enemy long before it targeted Saddam Hussein. Latterly, Gaddafi had been less demonised than under Ronald Reagan, but Libya remained on the US State Department's list of terrorist states. The war in Iraq shattered Libya's assumptions regarding international relations. To the Libyans, it seemed a demonstration of American invincibility. Hitherto, Libya had been able to rely on the support of the European states, especially when the Clinton administration had shown a desire to intensify the sanctions. However, it now became evident to the Libyan regime that if France, Russia and Germany had been unable to prevent the invasion of Iraq, then this meant the unilateral power of the United States was without limit. According to Gaddafi, "When Bush has finished with Iraq, he'll turn on us. We shall see quickly enough whether Iran, Saudi Arabia and Libya will be targets. Then American policy will drop the veil. It will be colonialism over again.... Bush doesn't act logically. With him, you can't predict anything, so you have to be prepared for anything. Today no one is in a position to say 'I'll be a target' or 'I won't be a target'."[3] The war in Iraq inaugurated a period of uncertainty, which alarmed the Jamahiriya.[4]

Following the fall of Saddam Hussein's regime, the Libyan authorities reached the conclusion that the Bush administration's neo-conservatives had in their sights the overthrow of all nationalist and anti-Israeli Arab governments. Anxiety began to spread through the Libyan leadership.[5] The possibility that Saddam Hussein might be overthrown by force had become a reality of a highly alarming nature, since it left the Libyan regime uncertain whether or not it would be the next target. At the same time, a media campaign insinuating that the Libyan regime possessed a nuclear and ballistic capacity was reminiscent for the Libyans of the Bush administration's propaganda over Iraq's supposed WMD. Actually, the Libyan leadership had the feeling that the Bush administration's justification for the overthrow of Saddam Hussein could be applied equally to Libya: namely that Libya was developing a nuclear and chemical weapons programme, that Libya was a terrorist State, headed by an anti-Israeli dictator.

In all seriousness, the Libyan leadership believed that the Bush administration actually had a plan to "remodel" the Middle East. The imposition of democracy on Iraq appeared to be a stage along the road to the democratisation of the Arab world, and therefore — in Libya's view — towards its enfeeblement. Democratisation was regarded as a style of politics calculated to instil western values into the Middle East and therefore to put a stop to its "struggle against the State of Israel".[6] In Libya's view, there was no doubt that the Bush administration policy priority was Israel's security, and therefore the overthrow of all regimes with military programmes sufficient to threaten Israel.

The apprehensions of the Libyans were aroused not only by their belief that the Bush administration's aim was to overthrow dictatorial Arab regimes but also by the appearance of an anti-regime Libyan "front" in the United States. The executive director of the "American-Libyan Freedom Alliance", Abdelrahim Saleh, wrote in these terms to President Bush: "The tragic events of September 11th proved beyond any doubt that freedom and democracy in the Arab world are as essential as ever for a secure America.... For more than thirty-four years, Libyans have been brutalized by the rule of the tyrant Muammar Gaddafi. Like Saddam, Gaddafi invaded a neighboring country, actively sought to acquire WMD, engaged in terrorism and regional conflicts, and used religion to justify his oppressive tactics. He is currently engaged in inciting hatred against coalition forces in Iraq.... As a result, the Libyan question must be at the top of your administration's agenda in the fight against terrorism. Like the Iraqis, the Libyans deserve a chance to put Gaddafi on public trial to answer for his heinous crimes against Libyans and non-Libyans."[7] In parallel with this letter, inflammatory investigations into the Gaddafi regime began to appear in the press.[8] Since little media attention had been paid to Libya in the 1990s, this further unsettled the regime, already worn out by a decade of sanctions.

The regime's reaction was immediate. On 19 December 2003, the White House announced that Colonel Gaddafi had made a high profile declaration that Libya's WMD programme had been halted and that its nuclear sites would be opened to IAEA inspections. Secret negotiations with Libya had culminated in the desired result:

Today in Tripoli, the leader of Libya, Colonel Moammar al-Ghadafi, publicly confirmed his commitment to disclose and dismantle all weapons of mass destruction programs in his country. He has agreed immediately and unconditionally to allow inspectors from international organizations to enter Libya. These inspectors will render an accounting of all nuclear, chemical and biological weapons programs and will help oversee their elimination.... Talks leading to this announcement began about nine months ago, when Prime Minister Tony Blair and I were contacted through personal envoys by Colonel Ghadafi. He communicated to us his willingness to make a decisive change in the policy of his government. At the direction of Colonel Ghadafi, himself, Libyan officials have provided American and British officers with documentation on that country's chemical, biological, nuclear and ballistic missile programs and activities. Our experts in these fields have met directly with Libyan officials to learn additional details.... With today's announcement by its leader, Libya has begun the process of rejoining the community of nations. And Colonel Ghadafi knows the way forward. Libya should carry out the commitments announced today. Libya should also fully engage in the war against terror.... As the Libyan government takes these essential steps and demonstrates its seriousness, its good faith will be returned. Libya can regain a secure and respected place among the nations, and over time, achieve far better relations with the United States. The Libyan people are heirs to an ancient and respected culture, and their country lies at the center of a vital region. As Libya becomes a more peaceful nation, it can be a source of stability in Africa and the Middle East.[9]

Confidential negotiations with Libya undertaken by the United States and the United Kingdom had led to this unexpected development. In the end Gaddafi's dramatic announcement had the appearance of a beneficial result of the war in Iraq. In truth, Libya had been searching since the suspension of the sanctions in 1999 for a way to reinstate itself fully in the international community. Since the events of 11 September 2001, Libya's desire for the resumption of normal relations with the United States had been evident. Nonetheless, Libya's announcement of the dismantling of its WMD facilities gave the impression of a victory for the Bush administration, at a time when Washington was coming under severe criticism for its Iraq policy. Libya served as the model of the peaceful "conversion" of a terrorist State!

The effort to resume normal relations with the United States

During 2000, the first signs of a rapprochement between Libya and the United States appeared.[10] Prior to the attacks of 11 September 2001, Libya had already taken steps calculated to soften its image.[11] In a further development, Washington granted permission to American oil companies to resume their links with Libya.[12] In February 2000, the US government allowed Conoco, Marathon and Amerada Hess to make contact with the Libyan authorities.[13] However, oil industry lobbying was not what made the Clinton administration shift its position. Clinton's reason for being inclined to allow a gradual US return to Libya was the threat that the United States could be outflanked by the return to Libya of the Russians and the Europeans. Nevertheless, many obstacles remained.

From the legal standpoint, it was necessary to wait for the verdict in the trial of the accused in the Lockerbie affair. On 31 January 2001, Abdel Basset Ali Maghrahi was found guilty, while Lamen Khalifa Fhima was acquitted. As far as Libya was concerned, this drew a line under the Lockerbie affair. The regime hoped that the United States would now end its hostility and permit the complete lifting of the sanctions. The verdict seemed, in fact, to have been prompted more by political considerations than it was reached on genuinely legal grounds. As Yahya Zoubir points out, the court's conclusion paved the way for the partial satisfaction of the oil lobby, which wished to resume their position in Libya, while continuing to put pressure on the regime to provide compensation for the victims.[14] In the words of President Bush: "the United States government will continue to put pressure on Libya to recognise its responsibility and agree to recompense the victims' families."[15]

The terrorist attacks against the United States on 11 September 2001 speeded up a reconciliation which was already in progress. During 2001, numerous meetings had taken place between leading Libyan figures and representatives of the United States and Britain. For the United States, the objective was to persuade the Libyan regime to admit its responsibility for the Lockerbie attack and to obtain compensation for the families of the victims. In return, Musa Kusa, formerly in charge of the external Revolutionary Committees, was permitted to meet British officials in order to discuss the presence of LIFG militants in London.[16] This Libyan Islamist organisation, which challenged the Jamahiriya, had already attracted the attention of President Bush. Its leader Anas el-Libi (whose birth name was Nazih Abdul Hamid al-Raghie) was a suspect in the bomb attacks against the American embassies in Tanzania and Kenya of 7 August 1998, which had left 224 dead and more than 5000 dead. The Libyan regime wanted the inclusion of the LIFG in the State Department's list of terrorist organisations, and at the same time wished to give the Bush administration a demonstration of the benefits it could draw from Libya's expertise in the area of anti-Islamist struggle.[17] However, even before this, the regime was anxious to respond to the demands of the State Department in the interests of removing obstacles to the re-establishment of diplomatic relations.

In 1999, Ronald E. Neumann laid down in some detail the objectives of American policy in regard to Libya: "US policy and policy goals vis-à-vis Libya have remained consistent through three Administrations. Our goals have been to end Libyan support for terrorism, prevent Tripoli's ability to obtain weapons of mass destruction and contain Qadhafi's regional ambitions. Since Lockerbie, we have added additional aims, including bringing the persons responsible to justice.... Faced by both UN and US sanctions, as well as with the attendant political isolation, Libya has reduced its support for terrorism and sought to distance itself from terrorist groups.... Libya has expelled the Abu Nidal Organization (ANO), uprooting its infrastructure and seeking to eliminate any ANO presence in Libya.... We recognize positive steps Libya has taken, a number remain on which Libya must act: we also seek clear and concrete Libyan support for the Peace Process, including the underlying principles of the Madrid process. In this regard, we are closely watching Libya's talks with EU and possible participation, with Israel and the Palestinian Authority, in the Barcelona Process. Looking to the future, we would like Libya to join and comply with certain international anti-terrorism conventions."[18] In 1999, the United States laid down its conditions for a rapprochement. Libya, however, took four years fully to respond.

To sum up, therefore, the global war against terror accelerated the regime's process of "conversion" owing to the fear of Gaddafi's Libya of being included in the "axis of evil". In parallel, as war was being threatened against Iraq, Libya agreed to secret negotiations with the Bush regime. The overthrow of Saddam Hussein's regime accelerated Libya's negotiations, which culminated in December 2003 with Gaddafi's announcement of the abandonment of his

WMD programme. At bottom, the Bush administration's interest in Libya was simple: to show that its war in Iraq was having beneficial effects in the struggle against the proliferation of Weapons of Mass Destruction.

The lifting of the United Nations sanctions, however, did not bring with it the end of the sanctions imposed by the United States. On 2 January 2003, George Bush once more extended the "state of national emergency in relation to Libya".[19] In other words, neither Gaddafi's acknowledgement of blame on Libya's behalf, nor the compensation paid to the victims, nor the announcement of the termination of Libya's WMD programme were sufficient to bring about the lifting of the American sanctions. However, there was a clearly a degree of reconciliation between Libya and the United States, which seemed highly likely to lead rapidly to the restoration of diplomatic relations. Before the American sanctions were lifted, however, the Bush administration wanted Libya to endorse the Middle East peace process — and therefore to recognise Israel — as well as taking a more active part in the struggle against terrorism. Paradoxically, in an international climate where terrorism was a major fear, Libya became a strategically important country in the struggle against terrorism.

When the sanctions were lifted, however, the democratic opposition to Gaddafi began to organise, fearing that it could become irrelevant in the light of the new convergence of interest between Libya and the United States. In March 2004, the democratic opposition published a document entitled "A vision of Libya's future", signed by 108 opposition figures, mostly resident in the United States.[20] This document demanded "the creation of institutional rule chosen by the people, ... the establishment of democratic principles, the rule of law and the independence of the judiciary, ... the combating of political, economic, administrative and social corruption, and the means of accounting and monitoring, without the misuse of power."

For those who opposed the Libyan regime, the rehabilitation of Libya seemed to sound the knell for hopes of democratic change.

The end of terrorist ambition

The "conversion" of the regime deprived the Libyan opposition of any hopes it might have entertained of an Iraqi-style termination to the Gaddafi regime, but also put an end to Libya's far-reaching policy of State terrorism. This had first been conceived in the early 1980s.[21] Libya's Anti-Imperialism Centre, set up in 1982 and known as the Mathaba International, was the international think-tank of terrorist policy. The centre formed the backbone of Libya's international terrorist policy, and explored areas of tension to find emerging markets for international terrorism. Since the Middle East itself was the sphere of influence of such regional powers as Syria and Iran, little scope remained there for Libya. The revolutionary regime therefore invested in new markets in South-East Asia, such as the Philippines, as well as in Africa and Latin America. Libyan agents offered training courses in guerrilla fighting and terrorism to many new movements. They also supported more established organisations, such as the IRA in Northern Ireland. The director of the Mathaba International was Musa Kusa, whose cultural sensitivity gave him the ability to strike up relationships with people of diverse origins.[22] In 1995 he became director of Libya's Organisation for External Security and continues to be one of the principal actors in the reintegration of Libya into the New World Order. After 11 September 2001, in a climate highly unfavourable to terrorism, the Mathaba International terminated its anti-imperialist activities, concentrating instead on the impact of globalisation on the international system.[23]

The "conversion" of the "Terrorist State" raises the issue of what precipitated this change. During the 1980s, two strategies were formulated to deal with Libya. These were military operations and economic sanctions, which might be applied separately or together. In a highly interesting article, Stephen D. Collins discusses the impact of

military operations against Libya on its support for international terrorism. Could it be that the 1986 bombing of the Bab al Aziziya complex brought about a cessation of Libya's support for terrorism? The
author's arguments are convincing: "Acts of terrorism supported or
sponsored by Libya appear to have reached a high point between 1984
and 1986. In the two-plus years preceding the US strike on Libya, the
Qaddafi regime was linked to 52 acts of terrorism. In a similar period
following the attack, just 19 incidents of Libya supported terrorism
were recorded: a decline of almost two thirds. Taking an even longer
perspective, in the 5 years before the attack Libya was deemed a supporter of 60 terrorist actions. The Qaddafi regime would be linked
to just 22 terrorist acts in the 5 years following Operation El Dorado
Canyon, again demonstrating a two-thirds reduction in terrorist actions. The decline in Libya terrorist activity in the years following the
US air strike might suggest, prima facie, that the Libyan case constitutes evidence of the efficacy of military force in combating state support of terrorism...The raid on Libya did appear to have two results.
Muammar Qaddafi curbed his anti-American, anti-Western rhetoric,
and Libya reduced its level of visibility in terrorist operations."[24] The
1986 bombings provoked a reaction from Libya, in the shape of the
Pan Am and UTA incidents of 1988 and 1989. However, Libyan support for anti-American terrorism came to a complete halt when the
international sanctions were imposed. Both the bombing of Libya and
the international sanctions demonstrate the weakness of the terrorist
policy adopted by Libya in the 1980s. The Libyan regime's ambitious
terrorist policy had reached its limits, in both military operations and
as an instrument of foreign policy.

Libya's status as an enemy of the United States dates from the
1980s. Under the Reagan presidency, the struggle against international terrorism acquired a new dimension with the explicit naming of five
States as providers of support to terrorist groups: Iran, North Korea,
Cuba, Nicaragua and Libya. Of these five countries, Gaddafi's Libya
swiftly became an obsession for American foreign policy, and the

United States began to consider military measures or the imposition of sanctions.[25] American policy towards Libya was formed on the basis of the regime's support for international terrorism. The demonisation of Colonel Gaddafi by the Reagan administration was also a policy of least cost, since it permitted the avoidance of confrontation with Iran and Syria, which were suspected of being the real authors of some acts of terrorism, such as the bombing of the UTA DC10.[26]

The Libyan regime's ambitious terrorist policy had been based on all round support for political and military organisations seen as struggling against imperialism, Zionism and neo-colonialism. In practical terms, this policy left Libya open to become a target for the hostility of the United States, Israel, the United Kingdom and France. Between 1978 and 1986, due to the rise in the price of oil, the Libyan regime had vast financial resources at its disposal. The cost of Libya's terrorist policy is hard to evaluate, but arms purchases during this period are estimated to have been of the order of 12 billion dollars.[27] The policy belonged to a period when Libya was seeking to provide itself with the accoutrements of military power. In addition to the construction of its terrorist infrastructure, the regime embarked on its WMD programme and imported conventional arms.

In the early 1970s, the Libyan regime attempted to acquire atomic weapons from China. After being rebuffed by the Chinese, the regime turned to the black market in order to put in place "the infrastructure of research and development" for its nuclear reactor at Tajura.[28] From the 1980s, the development of chemical weapons also got under way. The construction of the Rabta complex (known as Pharma 50), built by foreign private companies,[29] and then of Pharma 2000, near the town of Sebha, enabled the regime to produced chemical agents. The chemical weapons development programme continued during the sanctions, with the construction of the Tarhuna complex, once more with the assistance of private foreign companies. Many reports by American agencies detail the various ruses employed by the regime in order to put together the industrial infrastructure for chemical and biological weapons production.[30] On 19 December 2003, however, in return for the normalisation of its relations with the United States and the United Kingdom, the regime announced that all its WMD installations would be dismantled.

In the field of conventional weapons, the regime imported arms and military supplies in enormous quantities which were entirely disproportionate to the size of its security forces. In the early 1980s, France and the Soviet Union were the principal suppliers of tanks and combat aircraft. In 1986, Libya possessed an impressive total of 500 combat aircraft and 3000 tanks. Quantitatively, Libya became a leading regional military power, but in practice it was unable to use its military arsenal effectively. Libya did not have the necessary personnel, and brought in foreign experts to maintain — or even use — its armaments. The Libyan regime's military shortcomings were exposed during the war between Libya and Egypt in 1977, as well as after the American bombing in 1986 and during the conflict in Chad in 1987. Paradoxically, the over-equipped Libyan army even became an object of Gaddafi's suspicion. One observer commented: "the regime fears and distrusts the military and thus imposes conditions on it that limit its effectiveness."[31] Between 1992 and 2003, the international sanctions profoundly degraded the military resources for which Libya had paid the highest prices just a decade earlier.

The regime's construction of the terrorist infrastructure in the early 1980s was intended in the first place to eliminate the internal and external enemies of the Libyan Revolution. Libya's revolutionary policy in Africa openly targeted those African regimes that had given refuge to Libyan opposition figures, or established diplomatic relations with the State of Israel.[32] Later, the revolutionary regime, emboldened by the increase in oil prices, embarked on a policy of support for communist, separatist and fundamentalist revolutionary movements in Latin America (including Guatemala, San Salvador, Ecuador and Colombia) as well as in Asian countries such as Bangladesh and the Philippines. The Libyan revolutionary regime set up training camps,

and centres for instruction in the techniques of subversion and terrorism. (These included the so-called 7 April camp and those at Sidi Bilal,
Bin Gashir and Ras al Hilal). Members of more than thirty terrorist and
revolutionary movements passed through these camps between 1970
and 1993.[33] Finally, the support given by the regime to the Abu Nidal
Organisation — which had been responsible for the 27 December 1985
attacks at the Rome and Vienna airports — was for the US government
the real trigger for its policy of economic and military sanctions against
Libya. It is not easy to draw up a full roster of Libya's terrorist activities,
but it has been estimated that "more than thirty countries" have been
affected by "attacks sponsored by Libya".[34]

It was in this context that the idea of a "terrorist State" developed.
The concept in due course came to include a whole range of threats
identified by the national security policy of the United States.[35] The
Libyan regime later turned its experience of being a "terrorist State"
to the advantage of the "Global War on Terror" launched by the Bush
administration after the 11 September 2001 attacks. Libya was thus
able to capitalise on its terrorist past. 11 September 2001 provided
the regime with a historic opportunity to turn over a new leaf, giving
it the opportunity to go over to the "good" side: that of the allies in
the "War on Terror".

Joining the coalition in the "Global War on Terrorism"

Within the global struggle against terrorism, Libya joined the coalition of States at war with Islamism. In recent years, the regime had
acquired a certain level of expertise in regard to Islamism, a point
stressed by Musa Kusa, formerly in charge of the Revolutionary
Committtee for External Affairs, in his encounters with his western
counterparts. Due to its geographical position, and especially because
of Arab and Asian immigration, Libya had at its disposal considerable intelligence resources on Islamist networks. Arbitrary arrests of
Sudanese, Pakistanis, Algerians, Tunisians and others had enabled the
regime to furnish itself with information.

More recently, Libya had played a notable role in the resolution of an episode in which an Algerian Islamist group in the Sahara had taken European hostages. According to the Algerian press, the liberation of the fifteen hostages held by the Salafi Group for Preaching and Combat (GSPC) — including ten Germans, four Swiss citizens and a Dutchman — was the result of Libyan intervention. The Algerian authorities had wanted a thorough comb-out of the Illizi region, where the hostages were being held, but the European countries involved had opted instead to pay a ransom of between 15 and 20 million euros, via the mediation of Libya.[36] The visit by Abdelaziz Bouteflika to Tripoli on 15 May 2003 apparently paved the way for an agreement between Libya and Algeria on the GSPC hostages. The Algerian authorities agreed to provide a way out for the hostage takers by allowing them to leave Algeria for Libya once the hostages were freed. Libya appeared to be on the way to becoming a mediator in instances of the liberation of hostages held by Islamist groups. After Abu Nidal's expulsion, Libya had made continuing efforts to demonstrate its good will in relation to the struggle against terrorism. Only after its "conversion" to the New World Order was it removed from the list of countries which were "outposts of tyranny", according to the Bush administration.[37] In addition, the successful process of joining the allies against terrorism would enable Gaddafi more easily to eradicate Libya's own Islamist groups.

On 31 May 1998, Islamist groups based in the region of Benghazi staged an attempt to assassinate Colonel Gaddafi, whose convoy was ambushed in the region of Sidi Khalifa as he returned from a trip to Egypt. Gaddafi was wounded in the elbow, and three of his guards were killed.[38] The incident was symptomatic of the bloody nature of the conflict between the revolutionary regime and the Islamist opposition. Between 1995 and 1998, Islamist violence broke out in the Cyrenaica region,[39] giving the impression that the regime was on the verge of collapse. "While western policy-makers and the media seem fixated on the Islamic fundamentalist challenge in Algeria, the regime that totters on the brink of imminent collapse is Mu'ammar Qadhafi's Libya."[40] There were frequent clashes between the security forces and armed Islamic groups, and the regime savagely suppressed all who were suspected of being Islamists. In Gaddafi's view, these latter were a "virus", comparable to AIDS, which had to be fought, and were also a tool of imperialism and Zionism, which exploited them. The Islamists were seen as pawns in the hands of the British and the Americans.[41] Each side took its own view of the reason for the appearance of Islamic violence in Libya. Before its "conversion" the regime characterised the Islamists as a by-product of imperialism. On this view, they represented an alien force and their violence was imported. After the regime's "conversion", it linked the Islamists to Al-Qa'ida. The regime gave media coverage to the Islamist violence, exaggerating the threat in the hope of arousing attracting regional, or even international, solidarity. For the Islamist movements, on the other hand, the regime was regarded as "tyrannical", "oppressive", and "hostile to Islam". In the Islamists' eyes, the regime was founded on the usurpation of power and lacked legitimacy.[42] For this reason, the Islamic movements saw themselves as obliged to continue their struggle until the regime was overthrown, in order to install a new regime appropriate to the history of the "Libyan Muslims".

Violence against the regime has had a long history, but hitherto the non-Islamist Libyan opposition had been made up of a number of separate organisations, mainly based outside the country. The National Front for the Salvation of Libya (NFSL), founded in October 1981, advocated the overthrow of the regime by any means possible and its replacement with a national and democratic government. In 1985, an Islamic movement split off from it, from which were formed the present Islamic movements. In 1988, the Libyan Patriotic Army was established, made up of former prisoners of war in Chad. It was armed by Saddam Hussein, and was based in Chad until Idris Deby came to power, after which it decamped to the United States. The Libyan Movement for Change and Reform (LMCR), was established in 1994, formed of ex-members of the NFSL who took a different political direction. The Libyan National Alliance was the only opposition organisation able to bring together diverse ideologies, but it suffered a setback in 1993 when its leader Mansour al Kikhia disappeared after being kidnapped in Cairo.

The Islamist opposition emerged during the course of the 1980s. Its most visible components were the Muslim Brotherhood, Islamic Jihad and Takfir wa-l Hijra (anathema and exile).[43] These organisations were ruthlessly suppressed by the regime. For example, in 1989, nine members of Islamic Jihad were hanged after attempting to assassinate a number of Soviet advisers in Tobruk. During the 1990s, the regime's clampdown led to the radicalisation of the Islamic movement. At this time one of the Islamic organisations, the Libyan Islamic Fighting Group, had taken up arms against the regime. It declared a jihad against the government, and carried out a number of guerrilla actions in Cyrenaica, which led to the imposition of a state of emergency on the town of Derna.[44] For the first time since the coup of 1969, Libya's revolutionary regime was obliged to confront armed opposition inside the country.

Since the establishment of the Jamahiriya, the nature of the threats it has faced has undergone constant change. Throughout its first three decades, the Jamahiriya was in a constant state of conflict, starting with the war with Egypt in 1977, and continuing with the war in Chad in 1987 as well as its repeated confrontations with the United States.[45] The 1990s, however, were marked by new forms of violence, as is illustrated by the formation of small Islamist guerrilla groups within the country. The regime's wide experience of conflict had enabled it to develop an expertise in the control of violence. At the same time, the expansion of the Islamist violence in Cyrenaica represented a serious challenge for the regime, especially as it emerged in the historic birthplace of the Sanusiya, Libya's founding dynasty.

The appearance of Islamist guerrillas

Between 1995 and 1998, the level of tension with the Islamists aroused fears of a lurch into generalised armed conflict. In 1994, however, Colonel Gaddafi took steps to forestall the possibility of a Islamic political challenge by declaring the Jamahiriya's adherence to Shari'a law. It must be said that in the 1980s, his practice of interpreting the Quran had earned him criticism from the Muslim Brotherhood. In the course of a debate, Gaddafi had declared: "I adhere to the Shari'a as a source of positive law, in the same way as Roman law, the Code Napoleon, and all the other law developed by French, Italian, English or Muslim jurists." When a Sheikh asked him to clarify whether his interpretation contradicted the Quran, Gaddafi replied: "If one of you were to say to me, for example, 'The Green book is against the faith,' then I would behave like Ataturk did. In other words, you'll end up one day by annoying me, and then I'll say: 'Take the Green Book, throw it into the fire, and bring me the Red Book!' Bring it, I shall say. We shall have Marxism, with all that this would mean! You don't want the Green Book, a book written by a Muslim; you don't want the Muslims to provide a solution for our economic and political problems.... Fine, tear up the Green Book. And if we have to take up atheism, it is because you have behaved like fanatics, and you want to dictate our conduct in the name of religion."[46] Up to then, the confrontation between the Islamists and Gaddafi's regime had been limited to controversy between the Guide of the Revolution and the "ulema" (doctors of religion) over the right to interpret the Quran. In 1978, Gaddafi linked his political programme to the Quran. However, he accorded to himself a right to reinterpret the sacred text, a process for which he used the term "ijtihad". This greatly upset the ulema, who understood the dangers inherent in a mystical and socialist interpretation of the Quran.[47] By weakening the authority of the ulema, Gaddafi was setting himself up as a guide for Muslims. He also described the guardians of the revolution — the "Revolutionary Committees" — as "soldiers of God". Challenges to the regime throughout the 1990s in the name of the restoration of authentic Islam led to the introduction of the Shari'a in 1994. Colonel Gaddafi sought to forestall critics of his "progressive" interpretation of the Quran, especially by forbidding polygamy on the basis of the Quran. "We must return to the Quran," he said in 1978, "as we find in it texts and principles leading to the best form of social organisation and especially for harmonious relations between men and women."[48] However, his introduction of Shari'a law was not enough to halt the rise of the armed fundamentalist organisations. Though regarded by some as a "pioneer of the Islamic revival",[49] Colonel Gaddafi continued to face — as did many other Arab regimes — an Islamic opposition whose weight might be judged by the thousands of political prisoners he held.

The Libyan Islamic Fighting Group

In 1995, the Libyan Islamic Fighting Group (Al-Jama'a al-Islamiya al-Muqatila bi-Libya) made its first appearance. Its founding members were Sheikh Abu Yahya, Anas al-Libi (Nazih Abdul Hamid al-Raghie), Abu Bakr al-Sharif, Salah Fathi bin Suleiman (Abu Abdul Rahman al-Hattab). Between 1995 and 1998, the LIFG had around 2500 members, of whom many were former mujahidin with experience in Afghanistan. In 1996, it came to public attention with its attempt on the life of Colonel Gaddafi, and somewhat eclipsed the other Libyan Islamist groups. The strength of the LIFG lay especially in its connections. The ramifications of its network kept it in contact with other Islamist groups in North Africa and in Egypt.

The LIFG asserted the legitimacy of its jihad against Gaddafi's regime on the grounds of the plight of the Libyan Muslims. In an interview given in 1996, a spokesman, Abu Bakr al-Sharif, advanced its argument as follows: "There is no doubt that the tragic situation which is hurting Libyan society is not hidden from any person with even the least concern for the situation of the Muslim. So, the absence of the Islamic regime — which is a guarantor for the achievement of salvation and peace in this world and the next — is what brought us to this situation. Qaddafi, as a ruler who has been forced over the necks of the Muslims in Libya in order to achieve the interests of the enemies of our Nation, has fulfilled the role which has been expected from him to the letter. This role required him to break the rules of Islam and its symbols within the minds of the people and everyday lives.... Indeed, Qaddafi began from early on to constrict the spirit of the Muslim Libyan youth inside and outside Libya, and began to kill every person who even thinks of doing some positive and fruitful work to confine his evil and to arrest his corruption. It did not matter to him whether these reformers worked in peace or rose in arms against him".[50] For the LIFG, the direction in which the regime was moving had to be halted, as it was profoundly corrupting Libyan youth: "We are convinced that a regime such as Qaddafi's can present justifications for its actions. However, it went further, adding to these practices which create a realisation amongst the youth of the necessity to fight the armed evil with the armed good. Indeed, scaffolds for hanging Muslims have been erected in the parks, university grounds, and various areas since long ago, in order to hang the choicest children of our country. Then elements named revolutionary committees overtook the mosques, the schools, the colleges, and various organisations, until it became a familiar matter in Libya to see a student giving orders."

The LIFG spokesman was also able to invoked the justification of religious revivalism: "The most important achievement of the LIFG is the bringing back to life an overlooked requirement and a dead Sunnah. I mean, by the fight against the apostates and traitors. It also revived the hope — with the help of Allah — in the spirits which had been overcome with hopelessness and fear which had been created by the regime through entrenched means. For this reason, the popular sentiments of the people have become clear on the side of the LIFG and this is exemplified in the offer of information with respect to the movements of this regime, or the offer of different types of assistance to the mujahidin. Furthermore, the LIFG has shown the true face of the fight, that it is a creedal fight between truth and falsehood, and these are first steps in the path of correct change." Between 1995 and 1998, the LIFG carried out guerrilla operations against the security forces in the Benghazi region, prompting a salutary response on the part of the regime in the form of bombing raids on the mountainous regions of Jebel al-Akhdar where the militants had their hideouts.

The spokesperson of the LIFG described Gaddafi's reaction as "hysterical": "The regime is passing through a phase of unprecedented hysteria and is massing all its military force to attempt to annihilate the LIFG. Libyans have not bombed their own country since the Italian occupation. But we are witnessing today the Libyan airforce bombing mujahidin positions in the Jebel al-Akhdar, the heart of the anti-Italian resistance. This area is today one of the many strong points of the LIFG. Meanwhile, Gaddafi attempts to conceal from public opinion the real nature of these clashes by disguising his military offensives as raids on drug traffickers or the like. At the present moment, he has 10,000 troops in the region, including Serbian troops from the former Yugoslavia."[51]

The LIFG certainly had influence over the small businessmen, and the LIFG's rhetoric on corruption found ready ears among the population: "As for the economic front, you can talk without a second thought about the corruption. There is confiscation of people's money with no justification, the withholding of salaries from the employees, the black market which is run by some of Qaddafi's stooges, and finally what are called the cleansing committees which on the face appear useful, but beneath the surface employ torture against innocent members of the public. The regime claims that these committees were formed to fight corruption in government, yet in reality they are nothing but new tools to enforce the iron fist and the legal robbery under the veil of correction. In addition to this is the squandering of Muslim wealth in areas which only serve the madness of Qaddafi and his love for fame."[52]

Between 1995 and 1998, a major security operation was carried out in the Jebel al-Akhdar region. Road blocks were set up every 10 kilometres, for the security forces to check the identity of all the occupants. The authorities put up posters at hotels and travel agencies showing the faces of the wanted leaders of the armed groups together with information about them. From these details, it appeared that on average the wanted men were around thirty years of age, and that they tended to be university graduates. They were listed as "terrorists" belonging to the Islamic Martyrs Movement and the LIFG and were described as dangerous criminals in the service of Zionists and imperialists. The Jebel al-Akhdar region was where the Islamic organisations had originated. The frequent clashes which took place there had led to a clampdown by the Revolutionary Committees. Though soldiers were also stationed at the blockades, they were usually unarmed, due to the suspicion that they had links with the Islamists, and were always accompanied by armed militiamen in civilian clothes. In practice, the army was virtually excluded from the anti-Islamist struggle, which was undertaken by the Revolutionary Committees and the Jamahiriya Guard, who alone inspired real respect. In 1997, a traveller arriving from the Egyptian frontier would encounter almost every 20 kilometres a barricade manned by mixed units formed of soldiers, militiamen and police. The coastal towns were seen as secure and well controlled, but such towns as El Marj and Al Abyar, in Jebel al-Akhdar, were not safe for the representatives of the regime.

From 1995, the Islamist challenge had taken the form of a jihad, identifying from the outset its attitude to Gaddafi as one of military confrontation. In addition to attempts to assassinate officials of the Jamahiriya, which began in March 1996, a series of clashes took place in the Derna region between the security forces and a group of Islamists who had escaped from a prison in Benghazi. In July 1996, Mohammed el-Hami, the "Emir" (leader) of the Islamic Martyrs' Movement, mounted an ambush of the security forces, leaving 26 soldiers dead. The intensification of the jihad led to the formation of further Islamist organisations, which actually made easier the task of the security forces in tracking the guerrillas down. In 1997 and 1998, operations in Cyrenaica by the militias and the army seemed temporarily to have reduced the level of guerrilla activity.[53] Some Libyans regarded the actions of the guerrillas as legitimate. One informant, a student at the university in Benghazi, was adamant that the fighters should not be seen as criminals:

"They [the Islamists] are "Ahl al-Sunna" [People of the Right Path]. There are many of them in the countryside, and especially in the hills. They have declared the jihad against the Jamahiriya and slaughter all those who support it. They are the "Ahl al-Sunna" and their aim is to bring Islam back to Libya. They call themselves "mujahidin", like those in Algeria. It's not long since they declared their jihad against the Jamahiriya, so that is why there are roadblocks everywhere, but they are mostly in the neighbourhood of Derna. There are many of them there. But the Jamahiriya is very strong; it's not like the Algerian army." (Benghazi student, 1997-1998).

The "Ahl al-Sunna" appeared to enjoy a degree of popular sympathy. However — in contrast to the situation in Algeria where the Algerian Islamists detested the FLN State — the Jamahiriya seemed not to be seen by Libyans with Islamic sympathies as quite so rebarbative.[54] Though the informant just cited refused to condemn the actions of the Islamist guerrillas, he was also very receptive to Gaddafi's rhetoric on the imperialists' plan to destroy Libya as they had destroyed Algeria, through the instrumentalisation of the armed Islamic groups. The theme of the dismemberment of Libya by "foreign forces" was still a live issue, recalling the post-Second World War period when the British, the French and the Italians occupied and ran the country. However, the Islamist guerrilla movements only gained in credibility from the contempt for them displayed by the leadership of the Jamahiriya. This also applied to the other opposition organisations: the Front for the Salvation of Libya, the Libyan Movement for Change and Reform, the Libyan National Democratic Assembly and the National Front for the Salvation of Libya. This sentiment grew both as the result of the behaviour of the Revolutionary Committees and of the oppressive tactics of the security forces, who were reported, for

example, to have used heavy weapons to put an end to a mutiny at the
Bou Salem prison in Tripoli.[55] Opponents of the regime also deployed
the language of Islam and its criticism of rulers who deviate from the
"true path." This was illustrated by another informant (a graduate of
the University of Tripoli but an illicit trader by profession). Waiting
to leave Malta for Tripoli, in the full heat of summer, with his companions, he was standing in line to register the details of his purchases.
A senior Libyan official, together with his family, bypassed the queue
and succeeded in getting his bags through without a check. The young
Libyan took that as evidence of the hypocrisy of the leadership and in
particular of the members of the Revolutionary Committees — those
who were described by Gaddafi as "soldiers of God".

"In theory, the Guide of the Faithful (Qa'id el-Mu'minin) should help the Muslims. He should help to make their lives easier. This man, instead of taking us
through with him, uses his influence for his own family and his own benefit.
How has it come to his? Thanks be to God that He has let us see this."

This queue-jumping on the part of a senior official of the regime
prompted highly critical and explicit criticisms of the privileges of
the guardians of the Jamahiriya. It was also the signal for a generalised row between the insulted traders and the Maltese customs officials, whom they accused of giving undue preference to the Libyan
official. This trivial incident provided an insight into the anger of
some of Libya's younger generation, who gave expression in religious terms to their criticisms of a regime accused of appropriating
the benefits of the Revolution. The incident throws light on the fury
that erupted on 9 July 1996 at a football match in Tripoli when
Gaddafi's son Saadi intervened to oblige the referee to award a crucial goal to his favourite team, Al-Ahli.[56] An outbreak of banditry
was another factor in Libya that heightened the sensation of rebel-
lion. In the sanctions period, the targets were mainly foreigners,
with the result that Egyptian merchants made it a rule never to go to
Libya without an escort. Poverty was the main reason for the spread
of banditry, linked to the desperate situation of some families in

Cyrenaica. Nevertheless, banditry also had political overtones, since its principal target — besides foreigners — was State property.

There can be no understanding of violence in Cyrenaica, however, without going deeper into the history of the region. Cyrenaica was the cradle of the Sanusiya Brotherhood, whose founder, Mohammed Sanusi, built the first "zawiya" (a religious foundation attached to an Islamic brotherhood) in the town of El Bayda.[57] This inaugurated an annual gathering of Libya's zawiyas in the town which continues up to the present day.[58] In the early years of the 20th century, under the leadership of Omar el-Mukhtar, Jebel el-Akhdar was the centre of the Libyan resistance to Italian colonisation.[59] During the Second World War, Cyrenaica became a vast battlefield in which the Allied forces fought the Germans and the Italians. The fighting that took place resulted in the total destruction of some towns, such as Tobruk.[60] In 1951, following the independence of Libya under the monarchy of King Idris, subsistence became a real problem in a region that had been ravaged by military offensives and counter offensives, and where movement was still hampered by large devastated areas. At this apposite juncture, the nucleus of the Libyan army was established. In 1942, the Libyan Arab force had taken part in the battle of Derna-Tobruk on the side of the British. The Sanusi Legion, which had fought on the Allied side in the war, became one of the pillars of King Idris's monarchy. Libya's Nasserists were obsessively opposed to the Sanusi Kingdom in Cyrenaica, set up by the British on the model of Jordan. In 1969, after Gaddafi's coup, certain units of the army were violently antagonistic to those tribesmen who remained loyal to the King. The Revolutionary Command Council promoted schemes to build farms on the sites of the zawiyas in Jebel el-Akhdar.[61] After Gaddafi's address launching the "Popular Revolution" at Zuwara on 16 April 1973 — which placed Libya in a state of permanent tension — the regime continued to hunt down the Sanusi leaders. The Jamahiriya was proclaimed in 1977, and the Revolutionary Committees shut down the last small businesses in

Benghazi in 1979, thus depriving numerous Sanusi families of their livelihoods. The vehemence of the Islamists in this area was in part the result of this history of confrontation between Colonel Gaddafi's regime and local leaderships.

Islam was nevertheless in a very real sense part of the identity of the Jamahiriya, and the propagation of Islam in the world, and especially in sub-Saharan Africa, was a role the Jamahiriya took up with enthusiasm.[62] The "Jama'at ad-Da'wa al-Islami" (Society for the Call to Islam), whose headquarters was Tripoli's former Cathedral, had half a million members and was a powerful tool for the diffusion of the Islamic religion. It established the infrastructure appropriate for the propagation of the faith, taking its model from the zawiya tradition of the Brotherhoods. It built mosques, cultural centres, and radio stations broadcasting Islamic programmes, as well as undertaking the provision of health care, the distribution of free copies of the Quran and other measures. The Jama'at ad-Da'wa al-Islami was very active in the 1980s. In 1982 and 1983 so-called "Islamic conversion caravans" swept through West Africa. In the 1990s, however, its activity seemed to diminish. Following the pattern established by Sudan, Saudi Arabia and Egypt, the Jamahiriya's contribution to Islam took the form of the training of preachers, though in Libya's case the concentration was on Africa. In May 1997, in the northern Nigerian city of Kano, Colonel Gaddafi — though in the midst of his struggle against the sanctions — proclaimed the establishment of an African Muslim Front! The LIFG was consequently unable to widen its influence beyond its original base, which suggested that it would be unable to overthrow the regime.

The LIFG's strategic deficit

In the years between 1995 and 1998, the LIFG failed to escalate its programme of violent action into a pre-revolutionary situation. It did not succeed in generating a legitimate challenge capable of transcending tribal and regional affiliations. Though its violent actions were largely restricted to Cyrenaica, even there the LIFG did not succeed in creating the narrative necessary for the de-legitimisation of the regime: failing to gain acceptance for the idea that the Jamahiriya's oppressive policy was a continuation of the colonial Italian regime. How can the failure of the Libyan Islamic guerrilla movement be accounted for? Several factors combine to offer an explanation. First, the LIFG simply under-estimated the capacity of the regime to defend itself. Like the armed Islamic movements in Algeria, the LIFG mistook vulnerability for weakness. The Gaddafi regime was vulnerable, but this did not mean it was unable to strike back, as will be seen. In addition, when the LIFG launched its jihad, the regional context alarmed the Libyan population. The Libyan regime was able to point to the massacres of civilians in Algeria as an illustration of the "madness" of Islamic groups, and to warn of the danger that they might perpetrate such atrocities in Libya. The violence in Algeria served as a warning for Libya. The LIFG was also ideologically inarticulate — the Libyan Islamists were unable to present a coherent justification for their fight. Their traditional attack on the regime was framed in terms of concepts which attracted relatively little support, such as their denunciation of the regime as "oppressive", "illegitimate" or "corrupt". These scarcely constituted a novel platform, since other opposition movements — for example the National Front for the Salvation of Libya — had been employing them since 1981. All in all, the LIFG presented neither new insight into the nature of the regime, nor a credible alternative, let alone a utopian ideal capable of motivating the population. The LIGF's mobilising strategy remained hidebound by the traditional rhetoric of denunciation of the government.

The LIFG's inability to differentiate itself from the other opposition movements — except by its willingness to use violence — was compounded by the difficulty it experienced in linking the start of the violent campaign to a seminal incident capable of endowing the violence with legitimacy. The LIFG was unable to point to a distinct injustice (such as had been provided in Algeria by the calling off of the elections) capable of crystallising popular resentment against the regime. Neither did it have at its disposal the sentiment of humiliation caused by the presence of the American troops in Saudi Arabia, nor the spirit of resistance that followed the overthrow of Saddam Hussein in Iraq. The declaration of jihad in 1995 failed to arouse any generalised challenge. Finally, the regime's response proved to be fatal to the Islamists' armed revolt, which was to find out for itself, as had other Islamist guerrilla movements, the hidden strength of a threatened State.

The regime's response to armed revolt: repression,
decentralisation and liberalisation

In its strategy to overcome the Islamist guerrilla movement, the Jamahiriya enveloped Libya in a network of barricades manned by the Revolutionary Committees and the Jamahiriya Guard. Hitherto, only local militias and the army had manned roadblocks, both by day and at night, with the Revolutionary Committees and the Jamahiriya Guard only very rarely in evidence. The same was true in Tripolitania, where there were only token barricades whose purpose was solely to serve as reminder of the presence of the authorities. The joint deployment of the guardians of the Jamahiriya in Cyrenaica was not only a policy of strengthening the forces on the ground: it also reflected the regime's distrust of the local militias and the army. According to rumour, the Islamist guerrillas could be confident of being left alone if the roadblocks were manned by the military. Of course, roadblocks were not the only means of control. Transport companies and hotels were mainly run by former security agents, but their effectiveness was relative: foreigners were unable to evade the scrutiny of those who assisted the security services, while Libyans — who did not use these methods of travel — largely escaped observation. The division of the terrain enabled the Jamahiriya to prevent the violence from spilling over from one region into another, but was of no help in the surveillance of any particular region in which dissidence was breaking out. The regime's decision to use mercenaries was an acknowledgement of the existence of security problems.

Tribal allegiances were a real obstacle to Gaddafi's efforts to suppress the Islamist groups. The anti-Islamist struggle in Cyrenaica showed the limitations of the strategy of eradication employed by the security forces against the Islamists. The level of suppression was intense, and the Islamist leaders had to acknowledge that they were destabilised by it. Nevertheless, from 1995 to 1998, Cyrenaica remained unsafe for members of the Revolutionary Committees and the Jamahiriya Guard. The latter, if rumour was to be believed, had made use of mercenaries in its bloodiest military operations. "Mahmoud", originally from Tobruk, is a jeweller in Benghazi. He relayed the prevalent rumours:

"The air attacks in in Jebel Akhdar were carried out by Serbian and Cuban pilots. No Libyan would bomb villages in the Jebel. These were foreigners working for the Jamahiriya. Libya is one big barracks: we all have some family member with the Jamahiriya — even the Ahl al-Sunna have family in the army. I am from a military town [Tobruk] and we would never bomb people in the Jebel." (1998)

As the object of constant change, the Libyan army was unable to provide the security of a homogenous esprit de corps. Mainly drawn from the tribes, it reflected tribal allegiances rather than ideological affiliations. The distinction between the Islamists and the troops was sometimes tenuous, as the latter might well be members of the same tribes as the former, and were therefore to that extent effectively their allies. Recourse to mercenaries represented an attempt by the Jamahiriya to distance itself from the tribal allegiances that hindered its ability to clamp down effectively on the dissidents. Rumours that some sections of the military were giving assistance or even aid to the Islamic organisations in Cyrenaica added credence to this. The disarmament of the military in Cyrenaica by the Jamahiriya Guard, and the redeployment of combat units to frontier regions in the far south signalled that the military, more than the Islamists, were perceived as a threat to the regime. It was anomalous at a time when Libya was subject to sanctions on air transport that air power appeared to be the section of the armed forces that remained the most operational.[63] The use of mercenaries reinforced the image of Libya as a tribally based power that lacked popular support and was obliged to pay foreigners to defend it. Attention thus became focused on the "privatisation" of authority in Libya. This had become concentrated in the hands of members of Gaddafi's own tribe and the regime had been obliged — through the lack of a civil or military apparatus — to inaugurate security cooperation with other "sanctioned" states such as Serbia and Cuba in order to carry out its repressive functions.

In 1992, Gaddafi announced an administrative restructuring of the country into 1500 localities (mahallat), which were granted autonomous status. They were in theory free to set their own budgets and to provide security, and were entirely responsible for financial matters. Reliance on local administration was an admission of the limitations of the distributive functions of the Jamahiriya and an indication that it was having difficulty in keeping control of social change. Gaddafi clearly hoped by means of this administrative restructuring to undermine those tribal leaderships which felt themselves to be excluded from power, while at the same time providing those loyal to him with access to economic and financial resources. These new entities were in practice autonomous "micro-Jamahiriyas", run by regional figures who were in effect local Guides of the Revolution. According to Mansour Kikhia, the Al-Qaddafa clans associated with the government are structured into sub-tribes and sub-groups.[64]

This reinforcement of the clans around Colonel Gaddafi took place at the expense of the major towns of Libya's coastline, which nevertheless contained 80 per cent of the population. On the ground, the result of the move to administration at the local level was the introduction in 1996 of checkpoints at the entry of many small towns, which were meant to act as customs posts. Popular militias controlled security in their administrative districts. Neither Libyans nor foreign travellers took them seriously. Their inspections were amateurish and were carried out in rudimentary conditions. Youths stationed at each side of the road were supposed to lift the ropes that served as barriers to stop passing vehicles. Members of the Popular Committees were in charge:

"The Guide said the towns were free, and their inhabitants were in charge. The Committees were supposed to check people who travelled through the towns. That's how it was in all the towns. But here, because of the Ahl al-Sunna, the Committees had the help of the Jamahiriya Guard. Elsewhere, closer to Tripoli, the barriers were just a formality." (Benghazi Merchant, 1996)

Under the sanctions, the autonomy of the towns fulfilled a triple purpose. First, it enabled Colonel Gaddafi to delegate the Libyan population's practical problems to the Basic People's Congresses by which the towns were run. Second, in terms of security, it helped to maintain the fragmentation of the terrain, at a time when social control had been lost and the violent Islamist campaign continued. Finally, it delegated the Jamahiriya's distributive function to local leaders. However, the decline of living standards under the sanctions and the extent of the Islamist challenge obliged the regime to develop a more effective policy of social control. In 1998, the creation of the Political and Social Commands (Al-Qiyadat al-Sha'biya wa-l-Ijtima'iya)[65] — made up of tribal chieftains, notables and army officers of senior rank — was part of this process. The aim of these novel political structures was to diminish the authority of the Revolutionary Committees, now seen by the public as predators. At the same time, Gaddafi introduced new intermediary bodies able to reinforce his authority over those tribesmen critical of the direction taken by the Jamahiriya. For instance, in Misrata, Derna and Benghazi, "tribal associations" were set up, whose role was to re-organise and formalise tribal affiliations.[66] The brief of the Social and Political Commands was to revitalise local political life, which had up to that time been seen as entirely controlled by the Revolutionary Committees, to the detriment of the Basic Popular Congresses, which were in theory the people's representatives. The desire to reassert control at the local level represented a response to the slow erosion of the mechanisms of control exercised by "the people" of the Jamahiriya. Until recently, threats had come from opposition figures based abroad — presented as "stray dogs" to be put down. The Jamahiriya had been efficient in its ability to eliminate them. However, the Libyan regime seemed much less capable of confronting an armed opposition within the country.

The creation in 1998 of the Basic Popular Commands, made up partly of tribal chiefs and established throughout the country, signalled the appearance of a new tier of leadership. In contrast to the Revolutionary Committees, these figures neither bore the stigma of having been involved in the suppression of the Islamists in the period from 1995 to 1998, nor were they implicated in profiteering from the sanctions. By the same token, these new decision makers appeared able to re-impose the authority of the government at the local level. The directives addressed by Colonel Gaddafi to the Social and Political Commands provided a strong indication of the functions they had been conceived to fulfil: "The Commands are superior to all other bodies. They exist to reinforce the power of the masses. They are the body which controls the General People's Congress and the General People's Committee." The Commands were also intended to "control, motivate and direct the Basic Popular Congresses".[67] The establishment of this new political institution also represented a response to the complaints voiced during the previous decade over the monopolisation of power by the tribal leaders close to the government. The Basic Popular Commands were intended to broaden the spread base of tribes which supported the regime. However, the institutionalisation of tribal power, by way of the Basic Popular Commands, could not help but signal that the end of the revolutionary power of the regime was in sight. The process was not entirely unlike the Italian administration's reinvention of the tribes: in order to re-establish its authority, and in difficulty because of the Sanusi revolt, the colonial power brought into being new local intermediaries and gave them a degree of power.[68] The political transformations that took place in Libya resulted at least in part from apprehension of the Islamist threat, which led to changes in the political structures when the strategy of repression was no longer sufficient on its own. The decentralisation of power in Libya, through the augmentation of the power of local authorities, however, should not be allowed to conceal the difficulties these new authorities experienced in managing "in complete freedom" their economic and financial resources. In practice, the decentralisation of power was more concerned with spreading more widely the responsibility to deal with the Jamahiriya's problems. Through the involvement of local leaders in the management of power, the Guide of the Revolution hoped to deflect popular criticisms directed against the Revolutionary Committees, and against himself.

Hand in hand with the suppression of the Islamists went a policy of liberalisation on all fronts. From 1998, there was a genuine "cultural revolution" in the field of popular morals. Supplies of alcoholic drink proliferated in the towns, and a steady flow of prostitutes fetched up in the bars and hotels of the larger cities. The rigidity which had characterised social relations since the inception of the Jamahiriya seemed on the verge of falling apart. The ban on the consumption of alcohol and on prostitution had been a reaction to the supposed debauchery during the monarchy of King Idris. Gaddafi's rise to power was connected with a process of reaction to what had been perceived as a social tendency that was contrary to Islam and detrimental to the dignity of the Libyan people. The social rigidity promoted by Gaddafi was linked to the idea of purging society from the "defects accumulated under the monarchy". The results of this policy had quickly taken effect, so that Libyan society, under the yoke of revolutionary fervour, lapsed into impenetrable boredom. The saving grace was that the affluence of the Libyan people enabled them to discover the pleasures of the consumer society in Libya's neighbouring countries, and especially in Malta, which, for Libyan youth, became nothing less than a "garden of delights".

In tandem with this move towards the liberation of morals came the liberalisation of commerce. On 1 November 1998, the Central Bank devalued the Libyan dinar by 20 per cent, together with an announcement that further devaluations would follow. The major risk inherent in the devaluation of the dinar to a rate comparable with the black market was that the salaries paid to Libyan State officials would lose their real value. From April 1999, in a further move, the Central Bank introduced a dual rate of exchange, with one rate for individuals and another for commercial transactions. The Bank's intention was to cut the profit margins of both private and commercial importers. In May 1999, however, the Central Bank made a bid to expunge the black market by buying and selling dinars at a rate approaching that of the parallel currency market. In 1998, six dinars were required to purchase a dollar. By June 1999 — thanks to the Central Bank's efforts — a dollar cost three dinars, while by July, the rate had fallen to two. Private importers, merchants and the young "biznessa" saw their margins of operation disappear in a matter of weeks:

"At this rate, there won't be a black market any more by this summer. Fortunately, the price of goods won't change even if it costs a dollar to buy a dinar [the official rate was still three dollars to buy one dinar]. The problem is that we can't lower our prices, as we have had to buy our goods at high prices from private sellers. The dinar may fall, but we'll stick to our prices. It is true that the prices have gone up too much, but everything was calculated on the basis of the black market, at a time when the dollar cost three dinars. Now we wait and see how far it can go." (Young traders, 1998)

In practice those with foreign currency — including private individuals, tourists, and foreigners paid in hard currency — were able to change their money at the Central Bank at rates comparable to those on the black market. In political terms, this policy was part of an operation aimed at curbing the rising power of the private sector, whose independence in relation to the Jamahiriya had constantly increased. The Jamahiriya's recognition of private business had been reluctant and slow, on the excuse that business, which creates inequalities between one person and another, was contrary to Jamahiriya's philosophy. Faced by the looming impoverishment of the country, Gaddafi had already accepted the liberalisation of the retail sector in the later 1980s. However, the take-over of the private import sector, together with their control over the unofficial currency market, by the members of the Revolutionary Committees, entrepreneurs, and younger Libyans hankering after the consumer society, invited further criticisms of the direction in which the Jamahiriya was developing. Several times, Gaddafi publicly attacked the "speculators" accusing them of plundering the State. The installation of the "Purification Committees" in 1996 failed to produce the hoped for result. Presumably as the result of internal pressures — such as the effect of the sanctions on Libyan society and health care, the Islamist violence and tribal unrest — Gaddafi was prompted to utter threats against those who were profiting from the sanctions.

Colonel Gaddafi's hostility towards private enterprise was of long standing. He only gave his blessing to private businesses in 1988 because the oil crisis obliged him to introduce a package of measures in response to the recommendations of the International Monetary Fund. These included the liberalisation of trade, the abolition of subsidies on certain products (including tea and wheat) and permission for agricultural producers to sell their products in private markets. In 1990, a second batch of measures was announced, including the closure of bankrupt public enterprises, cuts in civil services numbers, and legal adjustments to permit foreign investment and give private companies access to public credit.[69] 1993 saw the launch of schemes to promote tourism and to facilitate the convertibility of the dinar. These reforms were not to succeed, however, and later, under the sanctions, the Libyan economy tended towards the appearance of the unofficial market.[70]

The social changes of the 1990s were incarnated by Tripoli's Rashid quarter. It became the liveliest and busiest part of Tripoli, where thousands of "biznessa" were active. With scant regard for the law, the young traders sold in the streets the consumer goods they had bought in Malta, originally from Turkey, Italy and above all Asia. The devaluation of the dinar pushed up their prices and threatened their businesses. The unification of the exchange rate promoted direct foreign investment in Libya, though it undermined the economic resources of the young "biznessa". The Rashid area was a microcosm of the social and economic changes which took place under the sanctions. More than 500 small businesses run by young "biznessa" sold consumer goods including sports clothes, counterfeit designer clothes, household electrical goods and video cassettes. For some Libyans of the younger generation, this market provided them with a lucrative activity, independent of the income of the State. Rashid was the heartland of unofficial capitalism. Its energy contrasted with the comparative somnolence of the city centre. The "Purification Committees" which patrolled the streets of the area very seldom halted the activities of the young businessmen. There were a number of reasons for the government's relative tolerance of the challenge posed by this anarchical activity, not least that it created jobs and brought dynamism to Tripoli.

The market acted as a safety valve. The crisis experienced by the "distributive State" brought with it a series of civil challenges mounted by a younger generation increasingly aware of the pleasures of the consumer society. Up to the end of the 1980s, Tripoli was almost entirely lacking in opportunities for leisure. The appearance of the Rashid market place, under the sanctions, broke the monotony of a capital city many of whose inhabitants were absentees. Tripoli had become, for many, a place for property investment rather than a city in which to live. Rumour had it that more houses were empty than were occupied. Previously, commercial activities had been restricted to the Casbah.[71] Today, however, only two "guilds", the jewellers and the traditional craftsmen, have remained in the old town. The sale of goods for mass consumption, intended for the "trendy" young, is now concentrated in Rashid, which has become Tripoli's new heart. The emergence of the new market has accompanied changes taking place within Tripolitanian society. Trainers and jeans have taken the place of traditional dress, and "rai" has displaced traditional music. Cafés and internet cafés — hitherto very unusual — have begun to spread and now serve as the new meeting places. Rashid can be seen as the resurgence of consumer society:

"Here we can buy everything we want — the latest trainers, Gucci sunglasses or Timberland T-shirts. All the global brands are here. Thousands of Libyans go to bring stuff from abroad to sell. You can even change money on the market. That's less attractive than it used to be now the exchange rate at the bank is the same as the unofficial rate." (Young traders, 1998)

All this has resulted from an adjustment in the attitude of the Jamahiriya's leaders. In response to the social and political tensions that resulted from the debilitation of the regime, and the feeling of being trapped that had ensued from the sanctions, Colonel Gaddafi put an end to the puritanism of his previous social policies. The emergence of the Islamists has obliged the regime to show greater flexibility in social affairs. The expansion of unofficial commerce took place took pace against this background. Rather than suppressing the young "biznessa", with the attendant risk that they might attach themselves to the Islamist cause, the government allowed them to amuse themselves and thus, incidentally, enabled the attractions of a tourist economy to make their appearance. To keep the youth of Tripoli happy, the Jamahiriya permitted the emergence of a hitherto unimaginable leisure industry. Whilst maintaining the fiction of the desire to develop tourism, new activities were allowed to appear:

"For two years now, lots of hotels have been built, and places to amuse yourself. How could we say we must have tourists, if there was nowhere for them to stay? Tourists have to have good conditions, and then there have to be things for them to do. There was nothing to do here in the evening before, but now it is beginning to liven up. We have cafés, we have ice cream parlours, there are bars and lots of hotels with girls. If tourists come, they can have a good time. We were behind Morocco and Tunisia, so we have to catch up." (Tripoli official, 1999)

The change in Tripoli was radical. Henceforth, prostitutes regularly appeared. Libyans, hitherto obliged because of the sanctions to make the sea voyage to Malta, began to discover the pleasures of the indulgent society at home. The expansion of prostitution was an indication of the extent of the social and political transformation within Libya, and was evidence of the regime's capacity to respond to demands made on it. The Islamists were not slow to notice the contradiction. The relaxation of morals also brought with it problems, as was shown by the affair of the "children of Benghazi". Two hundred children were hospitalised in France as a matter of urgency due to infections of the blood. Widespread rumours pointed to the risks of an explosion of AIDS due to the spread of prostitution. After first levelling accusations at "Zionism", the regime pinned the blame on foreigners working at the hospital. Such stratagems failed to reassure a wary population which was well acquainted with the tactic of identifying a scapegoat. In practice, the Benghazi affair led to sharper criticisms from the Islamists and from the tribal organisations. These saw the affair as an illustration of how the Jamahiriya was corrupting the Libyan people, and — worse still — endangering the lives of their children.

Conclusion

To sum up, between 11 September 2001 and the US-led invasion of Iraq, the regime in Libya underwent a process of "conversion". From being a "rogue State" attempting to obtain WMD, Libya became a respectable country, conscious of its new responsibilities in the struggle against "global terrorism". Paradoxically, Libya now aspired to become a model of "conversion" for others. Another reason for "conversion" was the regime's internal isolation. The Jamahiriya's legitimacy had become compromised, and it had aroused against itself the wrath of certain sections of society.[72]

The revolutionary regime has succeeded in overcoming the sanctions and has vanquished the Islamist challenge. Examination of how this was achieved throws light on the regime's inner mechanisms. In the first instance, the regime reacted to the Islamic dissidence not by mobilising "the people" in the face of the danger, but by turning to its most reliable security apparatus: the Revolutionary Committees and the Jamahiriya Guard. In contrast to the Algerian regime, the Libyan revolutionary regime did not choose to recruit militias from the people to win support for its struggle against the

Islamist guerrilla movement. Similarly, it refused to entrust the duty of preserving the nation from the Islamist peril to its armed forces. In general, the "republican" constituents of the nation were not mobilised in the trial of strength with the Islamists. Quite the reverse, in fact: the regime recruited foreign "mercenaries" to carry out air attacks, as the only way to maintain a distance between these operations and the "political community". Thus it could repress the insurgents while still calling on its most loyal apparatus of coercion to hunt down the Islamist groups. Lingering apprehension of collusion between Islamist rebels and the security forces was the reason for the use of mercenaries.

Another significant element is discernible in the light of the response of the regime when confronted by the Islamists. This was its capacity to initiate political reforms. The various initiatives of the revolutionary regime in the direction of decentralisation show that, far from being rigid, the regime can make real changes, refashion its alliances, and identify alternatives. The policies of the regime show real resourcefulness, which suggest a reason for its capacity to survive. Its determination to retain the monopoly over the legitimate use of force has not resulted in a blind use of violence, to the exclusion of political, social and economic measures, some of which have brought to bear unexpected resources. In all, the art of government in Libya lacks the refinement of the "adab sultaniya" of the Moroccan monarchy, and does not display the cunning of the Algerian military regime. Nevertheless, it displays a distinctive style of its own, not inferior to those of its North African neighbours. Almost like a "secret society", the regime uses mechanisms consciously based on a lack of transparency in its actions, secrecy in its decision-making, and the loyalty of its members. The revolutionary regime's communal spirit — in Arabic, "asabiya" — which links the leaders of the revolutionary regime with those who carry out its orders — is based on the imperative of unity as the alternative to collapse. But it also involves an efficient range of networks within the country able to subvert any challenge from the regime's opponents. The hidden structure of these networks sometimes emerges into view, and is most likely to be perceived by outside observers at times when the regime is faced by an existential threat and therefore needs to call on its deepest levels of support.

In fact, far from what might be expected from the image of Libya as an incoherent political system, paralysed by the irrationality of its Head of State, the regime has been able to assess the threats it faces and to formulate effective policies in response. As has been indicated, it was able — during the sanctions — to strengthen its internal alliances by conferring autonomy on the towns. It was also, with the construction of the Great Underground River, able to bring into play another effective political instrument.[73] The geography of water distribution in Libya reveals the Jamahiriya's deepest political structures. The Great River has brought into existence a policy of control over the water supply in a country where only three per cent of the land area lies outside the desert. In addition to underlining the symbolic role of the southern Sahara in the support of the coastal towns, Libya's water policy demonstrates the country's dependence on the water bearing strata of the Kufra region. Symbolically, the water policy shows that the country's life force springs from the Sahara and not from the coastal towns, which prosper on the efforts of the Jamahiriya as a whole!

In the last resort, however, the principal aspects of the Jamahiriya's situation draw attention to the failings of its ideology and of its political system. A new ideology is yet to be formulated. Gaddafi has been exposed to two conflicting tendencies since the official declaration in September 1998 of the abandonment of pan-Arabism. One of these is identified with the old-school revolutionaries, who have dreamed of the construction of a "United States of Africa" on the African continent. The other is that of the reformers, which has the support of Gaddafi's son, Seif el-Islam. Their plan is to link Libya to the West, making it a strategic economic partner of the United

States and of Europe. But can Libya really become a partner of the United States while Colonel Gaddafi continues to be its leader? And as a successor, would his son, Seif el-Islam not be the one most likely to perpetuate the Gaddafi style of government?

3

GADDAFI: HIS POWER AND POSITION

On 1 September 1969, in the small hours of the morning, radio Benghazi carried the following announcement: "Your armed forces have overthrown the reactionary regime, which was corrupt and backward.... Your heroic army has toppled and destroyed the idols.... Libya is henceforth free and sovereign.... It shall become the Arab Republic of Libya.... There will be no more oppression, abuse or injustice, no more masters and slaves: rather there shall be free brothers above whom shall fly the flag of brotherhood and equality.... Then we shall build our glory, revive our heritage and reclaim our dignity. Sons of the Bedouin, children of the desert, children of the ancient cities, children of the villages: it is time to begin our work, let us go forward!" Colonel Muammar Gaddafi had just overthrown the regime of King Idris, who was taking a holiday in Ankara. On 13 September, at the age of just 27, Gaddafi was appointed President of the Revolutionary Command Council.[1]

The young Gaddafi was an admirer of Egypt's President Nasser, and dreamed of taking up once more the torch of Arab nationalism, dimmed by the defeat of the Arabs in the war of 1967. The new Libyan regime lacked the military strength for this ambitious goal, however, and directed its immediate efforts towards the removal of the British and American military bases, established in 1953 and 1955 respectively, while embarking on the progressive nationalisation of Libya's oil resources. In the aftermath of the revolution, Libya proposed the union of Arab states — at various times attempting to involve Egypt, Sudan, Syria and Tunisia — with the aim of liberating Palestine and of overcoming the "inferiority complex of the Arabs" in the face of Israel. As Gaddafi put it: "We must understand that in order to re-cover the territory occupied in 1967, the Zionist military machine must be destroyed.... Having failed to do this, these countries [in the Middle East] have developed a complex of failure which paralyses all the Arabs."[2]

On 2 March 1977, Gaddafi announced that the "Jamahiriya" would replace the Libyan Arab Republic. This new entity — known in full as the Socialist People's Libyan Arab Jamahiriya — in theory allowed the people to govern directly through the intermediary of a General People's Congress, of which Gaddafi became Secretary General. In 1979, he resigned his official positions and wrote the Green Book, in which he expounded what he called the "Third Universal Theory be-tween capitalism and socialism". In 1989, Gaddafi proclaimed himself the Guide of the Revolution, and adopted the role of Head of State without official responsibilities. Following the imposition of the sanc-tions and the onset of internal problems in Libya, Gaddafi withdrew from the view of the international media. In September 2003, after the lifting of the sanctions, he re-emerged, a visibly older man, hav-ing now led Libya since 1969. Muammar Gaddafi, the revolutionary, the global dissident, now in his sixties, became a proponent of peace and began to entertain ambitions to become an international sage, after the model of Nelson Mandela or Mikhail Gorbachev. It cannot fail to be observed that the revolutionary fervour of Gaddafi's early days had dissipated, and that the hoped-for "just society" had never materialised.

In reality, following the precedent set by the monarchy of King Idris, the Jamahiriya had been transformed into a political instrument serving the interests of a single tribe — in this case the "Gaddafa" — and had contributed impressively to the enrichment of Gaddafi's family. This tribal closing of ranks within the regime fed the discontent of a population already irritated by the incomprehensibility of the Jamahiriya's policies and by the squandering of resources on a privileged minority. In February 2000, in a "revolutionary" speech to the General Congress of the People, the Guide of the Revolution, in angry mood, addressed these words to his audience: "Did the Revolution take place so that our oil income could be spent abroad on Kleenex? If so it was hardly worth forty years of sacrifice!" He went on to express his indignation that the institutions of the Jamahiriya had not succeeded in establishing their authority over the unofficial power centres which the people continued to regard as the real seats of authority. As he put it: "I want to hear no more of 'Tripoli says…' or 'Sirte' or 'Kufra'". In the eyes of the Libyan population, however, real power remained the perquisite of an opaque, unofficial and invisible administration. As the Libyan people saw it, this was based primarily on kinship. The "family of Gaddafi" — the Guide's own tribe and its allies — were undoubtedly regarded as the real government.[3]

The stability of revolutionary Libya depended on a number of factors. The first of these was Gaddafi's own nationalist spirit. The 1969 coup and the inauguration of the Jamahiriya were responses to the perception that the supposed deviations of the monarchist regime of King Idris (1951-1969). Libya's Arab nationalists had come to view the monarchical regime as morally decadent and politically subservient to the imperial powers. In theory, the new Libyan political system depended on a blend of political principles inspired by the direct democracies of the Communist world, the egalitarian spirit of Islam, and the revolutionary aspects of third-world theory.[4] In his Third Universal Theory, Gaddafi rejects democracy and pluralism in favour of political and economic egalitarianism.[5] Political parties were banned because "the party allows a minority to seize power which belongs to the people. To join a party is to betray the people: a party member is a traitor." The people were henceforth to express themselves through the vehicle of the Basic Popular Congresses.[6] In the sphere of economics, wage earners were to become "associates": as the Green Book says, "they are associated in the ownership of productive institutions."[7]

The bases of power

Studies of the regime of King Idris undertaken in the 1970s appear to indicate that its "fragile equilibrium", which had depended on "reconciliation of the demands of the urban notables with those of the tribal chiefs," collapsed after the emergence of a monetary economy, following the discovery of oil. The ties of personal solidarity, which had underlain the structures of patronage, were overturned. According to Rémy Leveau, the drift of population to the towns and the spread of education, together with the dissemination of new ideas from Radio Cairo, all served to accelerate this process.[8] The strength of the revolutionary regime was based on the satisfaction of nationalist aspirations, the distribution of wealth and goods, and on coercion. International sanctions (in force from 1992 to 2003) undermined the revolutionary regime by exposing the predatory practices of its officials. Nevertheless, in contrast to the monarchy of King Idris, the political system did not break down. Instead, after the model of the Algerian regime, it found ways to employ and exploit the new opportunities available after the events of 11 September 2001.

Following the 1969 coup, the process of constructing the institutions of the Libyan State can be divided schematically into four distinct periods. The first of these was from the 1969 coup itself up to the Zuwara speech of 1973. In this period, the machinery of power effectively consisted of four political institutions: the Revolutionary Command Council (RCC), the government, the army and the Arab Socialist Union. Policies were decided collectively by the members of the RCC, over which Gaddafi presided.[9] The promulgation of the constitution of the Libyan Arab Republic confirmed that the RCC would continue to be the highest authority of the Libyan Arab Republic. During this period, Libya embarked on a series of administrative, political and economic reforms, as well as making major changes in its foreign relations. The second period followed the Zuwara speech of 16 April 1973, when Gaddafi announced the establishment of the "Popular Committees", declaring as he did so that "the popular revolution begins today."[10] These early moves in the revolution were met with a resistance which later continued to grow: in addition to criticisms from other participants in the revolution over Gaddafi's monopolisation of control, there were regional policy failures as well as the threat of war with Egypt. The third period began in 1977, when the regime set up the "Revolutionary Committees", whose brief was to "direct and further" the aims of the revolution. According to Hervé Bleuchot, these were comparable to the "Red Guards" of the Chinese revolution. They furnished the regime with a new means of exercising authority, but one which tended to aggravate its tendency towards disregard of the rule of law through the exercise of arbitrary justice and the consequent violence which ensued.[11] The fourth period was that of the sanctions, from 1992 onwards.

From 1969 to 1977, the institutions set up by the revolutionary regime enabled it to withstand a number of coup attempts, and to fend off the threat of regional war. On the other hand, by the end of the 1970s, the popular revolution was unequivocally under the control of an authoritarian regime, where political, economic, military and diplomatic policies were entirely divorced from the political institutions which represented "the people". The government and the General People's Congress very rapidly transmuted into bodies which initially represented the RCC, and later came to reflect the "directives" of the Guide of the Revolution. The survival of this form of government remains to be explained, as well as the defences which enabled it to overcome so many difficulties. A key point is that the organs of coercion are the instruments of government central for the comprehension not only of the regime's ability to survive, but also of current developments.[12]

In theory, the basis of the "authority of the people" is the political system of "direct democracy". The people are meant to exercise their

authority through the Basic Popular Congresses, the Popular Committees, and the Professional Unions. In theory, all citizens become
members of the Basic Popular Congress in their electoral constituency.
Each Basic People's Congress delegates a Committee to take charge
of its affairs. The 600 Basic People's Congresses, the Popular Committees and the Professional Unions meet in a national Conference
which chooses the members of the General People's Congress. This in
turn has a Popular Committee (effectively the Council of Ministers),
which implements the policies of the State, laid down in principle by
the recommendations of the Basic Popular Congresses. The Secretariat General includes a Secretary General (the Prime Minister), and
a number of Secretaries (Ministers). The General People's Congress
meets for two weeks once a year, in late November and early December. More than 1000 delegates take part. The Secretary General and
the General People's Congress choose the Secretaries (Ministers) who
collectively form the Popular Committee. This constitutes the executive body (the Cabinet). Within this structure, Gaddafi is the Guide of
the Revolution, and no longer has an official role.

In ideological terms, the political system expresses the determination to exclude any form of substitution for the "power of the people".
On this principle, the Jamahiriya's view is that "representation is an
imposture", since "a party represents only a part of the people, while
popular sovereignty is indivisible.... Political parties are the tribes
of modern times."[13] Authority is based on "local government", which
implements its policies through the Basic Popular Congresses, which
— according to the Guide of the Revolution — are "solely in pos-
session of authority and the power of decision". In reality, "direct
democracy", however, falls under the control of the Revolutionary
Committees. During the 1980s, the Revolutionary Committees became the bulwarks of the Jamahiriya. In the eyes of the population,
they were seen as mainly responsible for the regime's increasing
emphasis on security. Their function was the elimination of opposition, and the silencing of any challenge, whilst dictating to the Basic

Popular Committees the political directives they were to follow.[14] In May 1988, in one of his televised speeches, Colonel Gaddafi said their demands on the public had gone too far: "They have lost their way, they have inflicted damage and hurt. A revolutionary should not be an oppressor. I would prefer to be in a position to show the Committees' love for the masses." By the end of the 1990s, the 40,000 members of the Revolutionary Committees, together with the 40,000 soldiers of the Jamahiriya Guard, were the bedrock of Gaddafi's power.

The maintenance of authority

Redistribution. The Libyan revolutionary regime was based on its status as a "redistributive rentier State".[15] Above all, the legitimacy of the regime rested on the redistribution of riches and the resultant improvement in the standard of living. Its egalitarianism is only comprehensible when seen in relation to Libya's situation under the monarchy of King Idris. Under the monarchy, 94 per cent of the Libyan population was illiterate; there was not even one doctor; and infant mortality had reached a figure of 40 per cent. With GDP at 35 dollars per head from 1951 to 1959, Libya was regarded as one of the world's poorest countries.[16] By putting an end to the monarchy with his coup, and with his introduction of the "distributive State", Gaddafi was able to present himself as the benefactor of the people.[17] The nationalisation of the hydrocarbon industry produced a constantly increasing income and furnished the Libyan people with better living conditions in such fields as housing, health and education.[18]

Coercion. The regime's ability to survive is also a demonstration of the effectiveness of its organs of coercion. The Libyan regime displayed an ability to overcome a multiplicity of challenges, such as anticipated coups, Islamist opposition and the sanctions. This spoke volumes about the efficiency of the security apparatus.[19] The mechanisms of coercion fall into three categories: the army, the paramilitary forces and the security services. During the 1980s, the army took second place, whilst the paramilitary forces and the security services grew in strength. These latter institutions, buttressed by civil forces such as the Revolutionary Committees, were the pillars of the regime. The overlap between the organs of coercion and the tribal system accounts for the stability of the regime in the face of both interior and exterior disturbances.

In Gaddafi's revolutionary philosophy, Libya should remain in a "permanent state of tension". The Jamahiriya is committed to the theory of the "people in arms", with "every town ... transformed into a barracks, where the inhabitants are drilled every day," and is therefore committed to maintain the state of tension, using the Revolutionary Committees.[20] In 1995, in pursuit of this idea, Gaddafi declared the army dissolved, putting in its place popular brigades which were supposed to defend the nation against all forms of aggression. In practice this policy was part of a strategy to curtail the strength of the army which had been effective since the establishment of the Jamahiriya. Numerous coup attempts by army officers had reinforced the Jamhiriya leaders' suspicion of the armed forces, of which the oldest units had been formed under the monarchy.[21]

The emergence of the Revolutionary Committees in 1977, provided a bulwark of defence against the army, though — paradoxically — it was from the armed forces that Gaddafi himself had emerged. The regime had set up the so-called "Islamic Legion", but the military capacity of this body was limited, as its defeats in Chad indicated. The Legion's utility, in fact, lay more in regional destabilisation than in military conquest. Massive investment in the army in the 1980s, however, did not save it from defeat in Chad in 1987. The incapacity of the Libyan army was exacerbated by the American sanctions, and then by United Nations sanctions covering arms sales to Libya. In the political sphere, and within the hierarchy of the security forces, military men occupied a position inferior to the members of the Revolutionary Committees. The abortive coup of November 1993, by a group of captains from the Warfalla tribe, which formed a majority within the army, was an expression of the resentment felt by this tribal confederation, whose members regarded themselves as the historic protectors of the Gaddafa, Gaddafi's tribe. They saw themselves — not unjustifiably — as having been poorly rewarded for their services. The policy of weakening the army was also in practice related to a generalised hostility arising from suspicions of connivance between the army and the Islamic guerrillas in Cyrenaica, as has previously been suggested.

Under the sanctions, the revolutionary government closed ranks, and the role of the security apparatus came to be vital in the stability of the regime. In September 1993, those tribesmen who supported the government were deployed to form a security force that became one of the regime's mainstays. The intelligence and security apparatus consisted of a number of separate bodies. At the apex of the hierarchy was Gaddafi's personal intelligence organisation — the Maktab Ma'alumat al-Qa'id (the Guide's Information Office), headed by Ahmed Ramadan al-Asabia — which controlled the various security services. In overall charge of security was the Security Organisation of the Jamahiriya, run by Colonel Abdallah Sanusi. Under his leadership, Omar Gueidar headed up internal security, and external security was the brief of Yusuf Dibri, under whom Nasser Ali Ashur headed Foreign Special Operations. Within the internal security organisation, there were separate bodies: Military Intelligence (Istikhbarat Askaria) under Colonel Mustafa Kharrubi, Miliary Security, under Colonel Jumaa Bon Niran, the Security Brigades (Kata'ib al-Amn) officially commanded by Colonel Massud Abdul Hafiz al-Gaddafi, and the Revolutionary Guard.[22]

Major changes occurred during the 1993 restructuring of the security services, including the dismissal of Major Abdessalam Jalloud, the coordinator of the Revolutionary Committees, who had been seen as the number two person in the regime since the 1970s.[23] His replacement was Mohammed Amsied al-Majub al-Gaddafi. The suppression of the ideological organs of state and their replacement with mechanisms of repression threw light on the new challenges that faced the regime. The issue was no longer to persuade the Libyan people of the benefits of the revolution, but to suppress those who opposed it. This change of emphasis led to the reorganisation of the regime to give power to its most loyal tribal supporters. Under the sanctions, a new cohort of senior officials headed the State's security apparatus. What prompted the change in personnel was the fear of further coups, armed Islamist opposition, and the dwindling of "popular" support. The sanctions left the regime feeling vulnerable. The reorganisation of the security services corresponded to a wish to adapt the defence of the regime to new kinds of threat.

The rise in the power of the Revolutionary Guard (Al-Haras al-Thawri), was symbolic of the changes. The Revolutionary Guard consisted in the 1990s of about 40,000 men, led by new officers: Captain Ali Ibrahim al-Kilani, Captain Ahmed Kilani and Lieutenant Ahmed Awn. As a paramilitary force, the Revolutionary Guard had from the 1980s been crucial to the regime's security apparatus. At the close of the 1980s, the Revolutionary Guard, though militarily very well equipped, was only 2000 strong, with the majority of its members were from the Gaddafa tribe. With the decline of the army due to the international sanctions, the Guard's numbers rose to 40,000. They had become one of the key military forces of the regime.

The Security Brigades (Kata'ib al-Amn) — which were deployed in the major towns — were under the overall command of Colonel Khalifa Ahneish, the security supremo of the town of Sirte. The Security Brigades were a body particularly important to the regime's defence. Under the sanctions, the commanders of the Brigades were Colonel Hassan el-Kasseh for the city of Tripoli, and Colonel Souaib al-Farhani in Sebha. A unit of the Security Brigades under the command of Colonel Abu Qassem al-Kanka was specifically responsible for the security of the Head of State. The Brigades also took responsibility for ports, airports, frontiers and missile bases, as well as running the military police. These units formed the core of the regime's security system, and were — thanks to their ample financial resources and the quality of their military equipment — the pillar of the Jamahiriya. Colonel Gaddafi's concern during the revolutionary period of 1977 to 1989 was to replace the officials in charge of security with new incumbents who were both younger and less indoctrinated by Libya's "terrorist" history. Such veteran leaders as Colonel Abubaker Jaber Younes (the Commander in Chief of the armed forces) found themselves supplemented by new officers such as Massud Abdel Hafiz, Khalifa Ahneish al-Dourbashi al-Gaddafi, and Said Weydat al-Gaddafi. In 1995, Colonel Jumaa bin Niran replaced Khuwaylidi Hamidi at the Head of Military Security. As Mahmud al-Kikhia explains, under the sanctions the Libyan regime reconstructed itself on the basis of the tribesmen closest to the Gaddafa tribe.

The reorganisation of the security apparatus largely downplayed the army. For historic and political reasons, the army underwent irreversible changes under the Jamahiriya. In the 1970s, the regime's military model had been based on the concept of "the people under arms" (Al-Sha'ab al-Musallah). Colonel Gaddafi regarded the army with suspicion, and apprehension over coups d'état never went away. The army had been assigned the task of the destruction of the State of Israel. In practice, however, it was permanently under the control of paramilitary forces able to hold its power in check.[24] In February 1984, the General People's Congress proclaimed that women aged between 17 and 56 would henceforth be conscripted into the army on the same basis as men. The Libyan regime committed itself to a programme of arms acquisition out of proportion to its needs and capacities. The vast size of its arsenal gave rise to regional concerns, but also led to internal developments. The whole of Libya became a "barracks under the sky". However, the limitations of Libya's armed forces were revealed after the American bombing in 1986 with the result that they were further dismantled. In 1987, the popular militias, led by Major Khuwaylidi Hamidi, were elevated to a position superior to the army, which had fallen into were in disgrace after its defeats in Chad and its inability to prevent the American bombing.

The Libyan army also fell into decline because of the international sanctions, as it had no access to the means of maintaining its equipment.[25] Under the sanctions, the army, with its strength of 45,000 men, gradually lost the importance it had enjoyed in the 1970s and the early 1980s. In 1991, the Ministry of Defence was abolished. The army was not mobilised to combat the armed Islamic dissidents. Attempts at military coups between 1993 and 1995 plunged the army into disgrace, while the standing of the Revolutionary Guard and the regime's paramilitary defence forces rose. By the close of the sanctions period, the functions of the various paramilitary forces had diversified. The Revolutionary Guard was charged with the defence of the regime; the Republican Guard's duty was the defence of Gaddafi and his family; and the Security Brigades controlled the main towns. The oppressive role of the security apparatus was manifest. The growth of a feeling of vulnerability during the sanctions had led the Jamahiriya to fall back on its mechanisms of coercion.

The threats faced by the regime had led it to close ranks, relying on figures regarded by Gaddafi as trustworthy. The quality required was absolute loyalty, rather than ability. In the political sphere, such personalities as Ali Abdessalam Triki (known as "Mr Africa"), Ahmed Gaddaf ed-Dam (a cousin of Colonel Gaddafi), who was unofficially in charge of relations with Europe, and Mohammed Sherif (known as "Mr Islam") were regarded as the highest officials of the regime. Certain figures from the "old guard" were also important agents of the revolutionary regime. These included Mustafa al-Kharroubi, Mohammed Zuwayi (formerly Minister of Justice), Abdallah Sanusi (head of military security), Mohammed Mesrati (a security department official), and Khuwaylidi Hamidi (the head of the Revolutionary Committees). During this period, the senior security officials played a key role, and their real powers considerably exceeded their official duties. Before the sanctions period, officials of the Revolutionary Committees had been seen as the most reliable element within the political system. Set up in 1977 by Abdessalam Jalloud, then the number two man within the regime, the Revolutionary Committees — led by officials directly appointed by the Guide — functioned as a virtual political police force whose role was to back up the Basic Popular Committees. Their illicit activities both before and during the sanctions brought them into disrepute, but did not result in their demise. It was clear that the regime had played down its ideologically oriented institutions and had brought its organs of coercion to the fore. However, contrary to a received impression, the terrorisation of the population was no longer part of the repertoire of the Libyan regime. Instead, the process of government was founded on the basis of family links and regional affiliations. The Revolutionary Committees functioned as a kind of state militia in the service of Gaddafi's family. As it relocated the foundations of the State on the basis of the security organisations, the regime also assured itself of unconditional allegiance, through matrimonial alliances amongst the security officials. The system of marriages between the leaders' children was a guarantee of loyalty. For example, Khuwaylidi Hamidi, married his son, Khaled, to Aisha Gaddafi, and his daughter to Saadi Gaddafi, one of Colonel Gaddafi's sons.[26]

In the last resort, the stability of the revolutionary regime was based on coercion. Libya's "distributive State" provided itself in practice with a formidable security apparatus. There was no opposition of any kind within Libya between 1969 and 1993,[27] and therefore there were no challenges to the government and no complaints against it. This was not, however, solely due to the self-contained character of the "rentier State", whose income enabled it to forgo taxation and therefore to ignore demands for representation. The revolutionary regime was in practice able to subsist in relative peace, not only because it purchased "depoliticisation" with its policy of wealth distribution,[28] but also because of its ability to suppress dissent. The absence of challenges and demands was the result of a policy of the systematic elimination of

opposition figures, referred to by Gaddafi as "stray dogs". Under the
revolutionary regime, arbitrary arrests, torture and disappearances
dissuaded opponents inside Libya from expressing their views.[29] The
"redistribution of material goods to the masses" — made possible by
Libya's oil income — did not, however, render the regime entirely
immune to opposition movements.[30] Repression therefore played a
fundamental role in the perpetuation of the regime.

The tribes. Revolutionary Libya was founded on a vision of the "just
society" derived from a "tribal" political model. In the Green Book,
Gaddafi averred that the tribe was a "natural social protection" and, "on
the basis of its traditions, it guarantees social security to its members."
In contrast, he said, "the State is an artificial political, economic, and
sometimes military system, which has no link to human values." This
image of a society founded not on the State but on the tribe, "in the
image of the Zuwaya tribe", emerges from the idea of the just society,
as described by John Davis.[31] From this standpoint, the tribe is a family, which has become extended through procreation, and the nation
is a tribe further extended. The tribal vision of society is the product
of contemporary political transformations: Gaddafi's Libya is part of a
continuous process in which the Libyan State, ever since its independence in 1951, has continued to show the characteristics of its tribal nature. King Idris's monarchy's roots in the Islamic brotherhoods were
equally strongly influenced by the tribal confederations of Cyrenaica,
as has been shown by the historian Ali Abdullah Ahmida.[32]

    The Libyan State was formed from the amalgamation of three prov-
inces which had been autonomous since the 15th century: Fezzan,
Cyrenaica and Tripolitania.[33] The Italian colonial regime had occupied
all three provinces, but administered them separately, further em-
phasising their regional differences. Italy's colonial policy also led to
the incarceration of half the population in "concentration camps".[34]
The resistance of the tribes of Cyrenaica and the Sanusi brotherhood
did not save Sayyid Idris from being forced into a twenty year exile

in Egypt. In due course, King Idris's regional affiliation was deeply to influence his monarchy. Libya's capital was moved temporarily to El-Bayda, in the Cyrenaican region of Jebel Akhdar. In reaction to this regional bias, and to the perceived decline in the state of society under the monarchy, Gaddafi's revolutionary Libya committed itself to correct the monarchy's "decadence". As the Green Book explains, the revolution demanded "a process of radical change in the political, economic and social structure of human society. Its duty is to destroy a corrupt society in order to construct a new and just order."[35]

Historically, Gaddafi's affiliation was to a small tribe which had migrated from Cyrenaica to the region of Sirte in the 19th century. Under Idris's monarchy the members of the "Gaddafa" were permitted to enlist in the armed forces, but not in the prestigious Cyrenaica Defence Force, which was restricted to members of the Sanusi Confederation. In 1969, Gaddafi's seizure of power elevated the members of his tribe and its affiliated clans to key positions in the State. Two other large tribes were similarly included in this process: the Warfalla (with whom the Gaddafa had blood ties) and the Maghariba. Many senior officials came from these two tribes, such as Major Abdessalam Jalloud and Ali Rifi al-Sharfi. The Warfalla confederation in fact constituted the majority of the army. From the historical point of view, this confederation had been seen as the protectors of the Gaddafa. However, after the attempted coup of 1993, carried out by Warfalla officers of the rank of captain, the regime placed its reliance entirely on members of the clans which made up the Gaddafa itself. Each year, Colonel Gaddafi summons tribal leaders to El-Bayda to renew their act of allegiance to him. The authority of the tribes is a taboo subject in Libya. The leadership of the regime denies that the tribes have any part to play in government. It cannot escape attention, however, that within the key political structures — the army, the Revolutionary Guard, and the Revolutionary Committees — all those tribes which have offered their allegiance are represented. The tribes and the clans

play an essential role in security, guaranteeing the stability and continuity of the regime.[36]

Under the sanctions, the revolutionary regime's institutions of
government were undermined. The highest political authority, the
General People's Congress, was not the organ it was supposed to be.
Its members approved the Guide's directives and stuck to a line that
enabled them to agree with him. Meanwhile, the Revolutionary Committees evolved into predators who plundered the State's resources.
The signs of such a change were clear. Under the sanctions, the pre-
dilections of the Revolutionary Committees were obvious. Financial
speculation, the illegal importation of luxury cars and the establishment of offshore companies were all part of their transformation into
a kind of Mafia. They even began to look like gangsters, at the wheels
of their BMW cars, dressed in leather jackets and carrying automatic
pistols. Under the sanctions, an "economy of plunder" developed
which harmed the Libyan people more than it did the regime, though
the regime gave the impression of having run out of steam. No longer
able to deploy its revolutionary rhetoric, isolated by sanctions, and
accused of international terrorism, the regime had lost the support of
the masses and was run by ministers with no rights or responsibilities.
It held on during the sanctions years only thanks to the tribal solidarity which backed up the government. Mansour Kikhia comments:
"There are a large number of Gaddafa junior officers, headed by a
core of colonels who are individually and jointly responsible for the
preservation of the regime. Most prominent among them are Ahmad
Qathaf al Damm, Masoud Abdul-Fatih, Misbah Abdul Hafith, Khalifa
Ihneish, Omar Ishkal, Al Barani Ishkal, Omran Atiatallah al Qaddafi,
Imhamad Mahmoud Al Qaddafi, Khamis Masoud Al Qaddafi, Saad
Masoud Al Qathaf, Hassan al Kabir Qaddafi. Until April 1995 the
central sector (Sirte) was under the command of Khalifa Ihneish, the
southern sector (Sebha) under Colonel Masoud Abdul Hafith, the
Benghazi sector under Misbah Abdul Hafith and the Tobrouk sector
under Ahmad Qaddafi al Damm. A failed coup attempt in February

1995 prompted Qaddafi to make changes that gave his cousins even more encompassing power. Ahmad Qathaf al Damm's territory was expanded to include all of the Cyrenaica. Khalifa Ihneish was appointed the commander of armaments and munitions, Masoud Abdoul Hafith was promoted to commanding officer of military security in Libya, and Al Barani Ishkal was assigned to command domestic military security."[37] It was this process of the tribalisation of the government that helped it to survive.

The family. Gaddafi's children play a role of the highest importance in politics, foreign policy and the economy. In this way, Colonel Gaddafi's third son Seif el-Islam has promoted an image of himself as the probable successor. Since 1999, he has made efforts through his "Gaddafi International Foundation for Charitable Associations (GIFCA)[38] to improve Libya's profile on the international scene. He was the real supremo behind the scenes in the negotiations over compensation for the families of the victims of the downed aircraft at Lockerbie and in Niger. Following the suspension of the sanctions in April 1999, his importance has not ceased to grow. He represents the faction within the Libyan regime whose aim is to put an end to Libya's pan-Arabist ambitions, which have brought the country only problems. He had close ties with the former Prime Minister, Shukri Ghanem, and the security services chief Musa Kusa, and has had a degree of success in changing the direction of Libyan policy towards reconciliation with the western countries. Fathi Ben Shatuwan, Minister of Energy, and Mohammed Ali Hujj, Minister of Finance, are seen as associates of Seif el-Islam. Another Gaddafi son, Saadi — the second son of the Guide, nicknamed "Libya's Zidane" — is a football fanatic and takes an interest in sport in general. He is also the president of Libya's Automobile Club. His influence makes itself felt more in the world of business than that of politics or foreign policy. He is viewed as Italy's man in Libya because of his close links with Fiat and its subsidiaries. He was still, as of May 2006, a football player in Serie A of the Italian

League, but also finds time to manage Libya's investments in Italian companies. Mohammed Gaddafi, whose mother was Gaddafi's first wife, Aisha, is Gaddafi's eldest son. He is discreet and reserved, but is regarded as Libya's telecommunications supremo. Chinese corporations have singled him out as their preferred interlocutor for negotiations with Libya. In total contrast to Seif el-Islam, he rarely takes up political or diplomatic positions. Finally Aisha, Gaddafi's daughter, has long been regarded as her father's mouthpiece in foreign policy. She organises international conferences, and had no hesitation, during the sanctions, in speaking out on political issues. She attracts the hostility of the Muslim Brotherhood and other Islamist movements because of her western dress and her high profile. In 2004, Aisha became a doctoral student at the Sorbonne and set up a humanitarian association. In contrast to her brothers, however, she has not achieved the status of an unavoidable intermediary for her father. More recently she has married and has taken up the veil, while abandoning her doctoral studies. However, while Gaddafi's family plays its part in the formation of political, economic and foreign policy, the Gaddafa tribe has an important role in supporting the government. Its closeness ensures that its members retain their positions within the strategic machinery of the Jamahiriya.

The high media profile of Gaddafi's children, each of whom, in their own way, has striven to transform Libya's image, has contributed to the "humanisation" of a regime long considered as a "terrorist State". For example, the role of each of his two sons has been well-defined: Seif el-Islam was in charge of external foreign affairs, while Saadi took care of social matters inside the country. Seif el-Islam is an advocate for Libya's changes of direction, while Saadi attempts to satisfy the aspirations of Libyan youth — which he to some extent personifies. Saadi's involvement in football is actually in a sense a political strategy, since the football stadium is one of the few places where political views can be openly expressed. He is president of the Libyan Football Federation and of the Ahli Club of Tripoli. Libya has not hitherto taken part in international competitions, but Saadi's ambition is to set up a football coaching centre in Tripoli intended to produce a team that will be able in due course to compete at the international level. His dream is to stage the African Football Cup in Libya. His commitment to football has led him to purchase shares in the Italian club, Juventus of Turin, owned by Fiat. Saadi has bought five per cent of the shares, and hopes to increase Libya's holding to 20 per cent. Saadi's policy has been a response to real aspirations on the part of Libya's younger generation.

Thus, the two sons have played an important part in ensuring Libya's visibility. Aisha, on the other hand, has feminised the regime, which is still dominated by the masculine figure of Gaddafi himself, notwithstanding his support for the emancipation of women and his personal guard of highly-trained female soldiers. An article which appeared in the London-based Saudi magazine al-Majallah brought down the Libyan regime's wrath on its Palestinian author, who declared his love for Aisha.[39] A highly controversial figure, she was a target for some Libyans, who accused her — because of her style — of failing to represent Muslims and Libyans. The children of the "Guide", through their extravagant behaviour, have enlivened Libyan society. They give a human touch to a regime seen as authoritarian and have indirectly allowed the topic of the succession to Gaddafi to be broached. From this point of view, Seif el-Islam, whose stock has risen consistently, appears to be the heir apparent. Through GIFCA, he has attempted to obtain the release of hostages held by Islamist groups such as that of Abu Sayyaf in the Philippines, and Amari Saifi (known as Aberrazak el-Para) in Algeria, in addition to negotiating compensation for the families of the Pan Am and UTA victims. As has been seen, his associates are opposed to Libya's continued involvement with the Arab states, and, together with the former Prime Minister, Shukri Ghanem, and the security supremo Musa Kusa, has worked to give Libya's policy a pro-western character. As a pro-western opponent of pan-Arabism, Seif el-Islam has made no secret of gathering around himself a group of leaders who would be able to help him secure his position in the event that he were to succeed his father. Colonel Gaddafi, of course, is still young for a Head of State, carries himself well, and seems not to intend to quit his post. There is no doubt that it is he who remains the Guide of the Revolution, and it remains to be seen in what direction he intends to take it.

Gaddafi's role: between the revolutionaries and the reformers

In practice, all policy decisions by political, economic and security officials hang on the directives of Colonel Gaddafi.[40] The Libyan State is incapacitated by the absence of a legitimate institution able to work in an organised way towards the formation of policy. In theory, according to Gaddafi's vision, the State should wither away so that "the people" can take their destiny directly in their own hands. Standing outside the institutions, Gaddafi sees his role as that of giving guidance to the revolution. But in this context, Libya's political and economic decision makers await his orders before acting. They take no initiatives, fearing condemnation by the Revolutionary Committees for failure to conform to the philosophy of the Guide as expressed in his speeches. The major difficulty is that the Guide's addresses are illogical, contradictory and ambiguous. They say one thing and then the opposite. This is why the advice given by the Basic Popular Committees to the General People's Congress exactly reflects the latest declaration of the Guide. Gaddafi constantly criticises the lack of courage shown by the delegates of the Basic Popular Committees, while encouraging them to make policy decisions. In his words, "I say to them, have fear of no-one, no-one is above you." But in an authoritarian and arbitrary system, no-one is willing to take the risk of taking even the smallest decision, at all levels of the political and economic structure, without knowing with certainty that the Guide will approve. Libya's political, economic and foreign policy failures — including the war in Africa, terrorism, and the United Nations sanctions — have resulted from the arbitrary nature of the decision making process. Any leader or official who dared to oppose such decisions, and their consequences for Libya, would be obliged to go into exile in order freely to express his views. The political institutions have never played any part making the policy of the Jamahiriya. Libyan public opinion is impossible to fathom. The Libyans have no channel through which to express themselves.[41]

The distribution of power in Libya depends on family, tribal and regional equilibria. There is no informal structure in control of the decision making process, such as the armed forces in Algeria, or the Makhzen in Morocco. Unofficial policy formation only occurs as the result of personal contact. The Jamahiriya has huge resources at its disposal thanks to the export of oil and gas. However, the income from hydrocarbons is not under the control of the political institutions. Part of this money is redistributed, in a manner which is entirely subject to the goodwill of Gaddafi's family. Historically, the Sanusi tribe of Cyrenaica has long dominated the Libyan government. The 1969 coup resulted in the introduction of a regime whose inclination was steadily to attenuate the power of any political institutions, movements or tribes capable of mounting a challenge to it. In exchange, Colonel Gaddafi installed a family and tribal network which would guarantee the stability and continuation of the regime. It is within this complex network that political, economic and foreign policy decisions are made. The process is an informal one, and brings into play figures from the various family branches, clans and tribes that control the Jamahiriya's crucial machinery.

The Libyan decision makers who are responsible for Libya's change of direction make up a narrow circle around Gaddafi. In the field of security, Musa Kusa, the head of the secret services and the former director of the Mathaba International, has been someone who has been able to persuade Colonel Gaddafi to modify his policies, when this has been necessary to ensure the regime's stability.[42] Other key names in the security area are Mohammed Mesrati (a senior security official), Abdallah Sanusi (head of military security), and Khuwaylidi Hamidi (head of the Revolutionary Committees), who is close to Gaddafi because of matrimonial links. Al Hadi Embrish, commander of the Rapid Intervention Brigades, has also risen rapidly within the political system.

In the economic sector, Abdallah Salem el-Badri has become a key figure in oil politics. Overall, while Abdallah Salem el-Badri remains the oil supremo, Musa Kusa has taken on the role of integrating Libya into the war against terror following 11 September 2001. After the invasion of Iraq and the escalation in the price of oil, Libya became useful to the Bush administration and to Europe. New faces were brought in at the time of the ministerial reshuffle of June 2003. Three substantial figures became central in the management of Libyan economic policy. These were the Prime Minister, Shukri Ghanem, and Abdallah Salem al-Badri, second in order of protocol, and Abdulhafid Zlitni, the head of the National Oil Corporation. The priority given to the re-launch of oil production after the lifting of the sanctions placed these figures in a strategic position in any negotiation with the Libyan government. In the field of foreign policy, figures such as Ahmed Gaddaf el-Dam, a cousin of Colonel Gaddafi, play a central role. He serves as a direct channel between foreign leaders and Gaddafi himself. Hamid el-Hudeyri, ambassador in Brussels, has been a negotiator between Libya and the Anglo-Saxon world. It was he who conceived the "gentlemen's agreements" with the ambassadors of the United States and Britain which precluded the possibility of further legal proceedings against the Libyan leadership. This facilitated the resumption of relations with Britain and the United States, which announced on 16 May 2006 that it was restoring full diplomatic relations with Libya.

Gaddafi's role in post-sanctions Libya has consisted of maintaining a balance between the various factions into which Libya's decision makers are divided. For instance, under the sanctions, the pan-Africanists exercised most influence over Gaddafi. However, after the suspension of the sanctions in April 1999 and then their definitive lifting in September 2003, pro-western officials had most success in engaging his attention. As to Gaddafi himself, his personal ambition is to become a "wise man" in Africa, dedicated to the cause of peace. His goal, in all seriousness, is to become, together with Nelson Mandela and Mikhail Gorbachev, an element within a troika of wise men at the service of the United Nations. Gaddafi's trip to Brussels, on 24 March 2004, was an illustration of his desire to present himself as an indispensable mediator between Africa and Europe. It must be pointed out, however, that such an ambition arouses mixed reactions.

The United States of Africa

There are two distinct schools of political thought within Gaddafi's entourage. One favours reform that tends in the direction of liberalisation, the opening up of the economy and the location of Libya within Europe's Mediterranean sphere. Gaddafi's son Seif el-Islam is a leading figure within this faction, and advocates revision of the Jamahiriya's policies. In the view of this tendency, Arab nationalism is responsible for the difficulties in which the states of the Middle East currently find themselves. Libya should amend its political direction, placing itself fully within the western camp led by the United States. In 2000, those who took this view were in a minority, and were outweighed by the "revolutionaries", in whose view Libya should continue to look towards Africa. Africa was the cradle of the Libyan revolutionaries. Within the Mathaba International, directed by Musa Kusa, Africa has always had a significant role. In the sanctions period, Libyan policy divided Africa into three sections. One of these, directed by Abdul Salem Zadmeh,[43] covered Central and West Africa and played a significant role in arming the Rwandan Patriotic Front. The second, run by Mohammed Abdallah Hijazi, was dedicated to Saharan Africa, and the third section was devoted to South Africa.[44] After the suspension of the sanctions, Africa became an important region for Libyan economic investment, within the framework of the African Union.[45]

After the suspension of the sanctions, Libya directed its foreign policy towards Africa, and not without success. In September 1999, at the extraordinary summit of the Organisation of African Union (OAU) in Sirte, Gaddafi launched his ambitious plan for a United States of Africa. Feeling let down by the Arabs and their lack of gratitude, he had turned once more to Africa. The backing given by the African states to the campaign for the suspension of the sanctions, which were in the event partially lifted by the United Nations in June 1998, induced Gaddafi to abandon the ideology of pan-Arabism and to espouse pan-Africanism in its place.[46] February 1998 saw the establishment of COMESSA (The Community of Sahel and Saharan States), whose goal was to organise and back up Libya's African policy. In the first instance, this grouping included Mali, Burkina Faso, Niger, Chad and Sudan. In April 1999, the Central African republic and Eritrea joined up. Then in February 2000, Djibouti, Senegal and the Gambia became members. COMESSA was re-named "CEN-SAD": the Community of the Sahel and the Sahara, with a budget of seven million dollars. Libya regained something of the energy it had thrown into foreign policy before the sanctions, but with the difference that Gaddafi sought to make his capital city the nerve-centre of peace in Africa, rather than of revolution.

At the OAU summit Gaddafi offered a constitution for the United States of Africa, setting out an ambitious plan for the development of the continent. "A collectivity which will be known as the United States of Africa," he said, "will be the historic solution for the continent." This would provide the solution for the problems of war and under-development: "As I see it, Africa is absolutely not a poor continent. Perhaps cash is lacking, but it has resources and raw materials. I regard Africa as a rich continent. However, the capitalist countries have put a veto on Africa. They don't want our continent to develop. They want to keep Africa as it is, in order to take away its raw materials."[47] The major turning point in Libya's African policy was the official renunciation of violence. The plan for a United States of the Sahel, formulated during the 1970s, had in fact depended on a revolutionary policy based on the overthrow of the regimes.[48] The present plan, however, was no longer conditional on liberation, but rather on cooperation. "In the era of national liberation, I struggled alongside Angola, Zimbabwe, South Africa, Namibia, Guinea-Bissau, Cap Verde, Algeria, Palestine.... But today, we can throw away our guns to work for peace and development. This is my role. War has had its day."[49]

The United States of Africa represented an opportunity to set up the infrastructure necessary to attract foreign investors, and for the creation of a fund for Africa, an African development bank, and a single currency. All this would have enabled Africa to engage with the IMF as a single interlocutor. Such a plan could have also offered a solution for all the frontier demarcation problems of Africa. Instead of seeking to amend frontier lines through conflict, with all the possibilities of foreign involvement that this implied, they should simply be abolished. According to Gaddafi: "If we took the decision that Africans should be free to travel and live in any country on the continent, we could get over the problem of frontiers. Africa is not like Europe. Europe is made up of nations. Africa is made up of tribes. The tribes were torn apart by the colonial countries. The "State" in Africa cannot survive, since it is artificial." From this perspective, the African nation would be better equipped to become a "United States" than would Europe. "In Africa, there is one race — the black race — united and composed of various tribes."[50] Gaddafi's vision was to expand to the scale of Africa as a whole one of the principles of the Jamahiriya, as developed in the Green Book: the abolition of the state. In February 2001, Gaddafi proclaimed that a major political step had been taken at the Sirte African Union summit, with the recognition of the Founding Charter of the African Union. In fact, the Charter had already been adopted in July 2000 at Lomé. The role of the Sirte summit was to speed up the process of integration needed to achieve African unity.[51]

Far from enthusing the Libyan "masses", however, Libya's African policies simply aroused sentiments of rejection against the country's African immigrants, who were seen as carriers of all the evils of the

continent, such as AIDS, poverty and violence. In reality, many feared
that the Jamahiriya was once more squandering its resources in an ill-
considered foreign policy venture with little relevance to Libya's economic reality. In addition, it harked back to a revolutionary past that
the Libyans were trying to forget. The revival of the African policy
contradicted the expectations of an urban society which aspired to
emulate the social model of western consumerism. Two representations of Africa seemed to be taking shape. The first was that of a
sub-Saharan Africa with a link to Libya, an idea which had enthused
the generation that had participated in Libya's independence. Given
the historical links between the Libyan zawiyas and the Sahelian and
Saharan populations, it could well be postulated that the élites of sub-
Saharan Africa had ties with Libya that could not be severed. Libya's
National Museum was a reminder that since Roman times, the most
renowned of Libya's tribes, the Garamantes, had derived its strength
from the Saharan hinterland. The supply of water to the coastal towns
from the construction of the Great Underground River was a further
indication of the crucial link which united the Libyans of the coast to
those of the Sahara. 94 per cent of the Libyan population lived in a
coastal strip 2000 kilometres long but only a few kilometres wide.
The second of these two representations, however, was that of Africa
as a source of trouble, associated with such undesirable phenomena
as war, AIDS and immigration, which Libya should seek to avoid. On
this view, it was towards Europe and to the link between the Maghreb
(the Arab West) and the Mashreq (the Arab East) that Libya should
turn. In contrast to the situation prevailing in the Maghreb countries,
Libya had no fear of the dilution of its sense of identity. Relationships with Europe were not a matter of identity politics. Libyans were
proud of speaking only Arabic, and of the obligation they placed on
foreigners to learn their language.

From the strictly diplomatic point of view, the African policy
has been a success. From the foundation of COMESSA, the African
States continued to sign up to the "United States of Africa" agenda. As

seen by Tripoli-based diplomats, Gaddafi has made good his African policy. African states have opened embassies in Tripoli, sometimes — as was the case with the Republic of the Comoros — entirely at Libya's expense. The resurgence of western foreign policy interest in Africa has been another factor leading African states to conclude that there was something to be said for the plan for a United States of Africa. It remains to be seen, however, how this policy will work out in practice, as Libya's internal unrest cast doubt on the viability of the development of links with Africa. Libya seems to have arrived at a crossroads. A major faction within the population is obsessed with the western model, and in particular that of the United States of America, as is shown by the sales of CDs of western music and English language textbooks. Another lobby, however, wants to keep the Libyan revolution on track. Colonel Gaddafi's goal has been to bring about a synthesis of these two factions, in which — though not without problems — he has enjoyed a measure of success.

Libya and the Euro-Med Partnership

On 27 April 2004, Colonel Gaddafi paid a historic visit to Brussels at the invitation of the European Commission. Since 1992, Gaddafi had been unable to travel to western states, because of various legal proceedings which had been instituted against him. Nonetheless, as Romano Prodi, the then President of the European Commission pointed out, "The European Union has no formal relations with Libya and the Commission has no delegation in Tripoli. However, Libya is a key country of the southern Mediterranean coast, as well as playing an important role in the continent of Africa. Libya has enjoyed observer status at the Barcelona Process since April 1999, having been invited for the first time to the Euro-Med Conference in Stuttgart. Subsequently, Libya was invited to become a full member of the Process. This required a formal approach in which Libya committed itself to accept all that had already been agreed within the Process, which was submitted to the Council."[52]

Europe's desire to integrate Libya into the Euro-Med Partnership was of long standing. Romano Prodi invited Colonel Gaddafi to Brussels in April 1999, as soon as the United Nations sanctions were suspended. The objective was to involve him in discussions over membership of the Euro-Mediterranean Partnership. However, this invitation prompted a lively discussion between Chris Patten, who was in charge of relations with the Mediterranean countries, and Javier Solana, responsible for the European Union's foreign policy and internal security. The two officials pointed out that Libya had not yet been cleared of the accusations brought against it. This false start in Europe was to exacerbate Colonel Gaddafi's language in regard to the prospect of association with Europe: "The European experiment is of no use to us ... the area known as North Africa should be Africanised. Either it will become part of Africa or it will be an anomaly, and will therefore have no future. As an inhabitant of North Africa, I have always rejected the Barcelona agreement, which regards North Africa as a part of the Middle East, with a vocation to integrate with Europe. This is a conspiracy against the integrity of the territory of Africa. They have said to me: the Barcelona agreement and cooperation with the European Union will be to Libya's advantage. They want to draw us in and to make use of us, through the Barcelona agreement, to dismember the African continent, stealing North Africa in order to join it to the European Union. This is unacceptable. In any case, look at what has already become of the Barcelona agreement. It is in a comatose condition and could well disappear."[53] In spite of all this, however, once the sanctions were lifted Gaddafi went to Brussels.

The change in direction is explicable in terms of the rise in power of the reformers and realists in the Jamahiriya, who want to attach Libya to its Mediterranean flank. In their view, Libya had lost its way in its African policy, and had wasted resources in an unequal struggle against "colonialism" and "imperialism" which in practice amounted to a battle for influence against France and the United Kingdom. The Euro-Med Partnership presents, in contrast, the opportunity for a rapprochement with these two former colonial powers in Africa. For the Libyan reformers, the realistic view is that Europe is Libya's main economic partner and the principal destination for Libya's oil and gas. This should be translated into political and diplomatic relations to match the level of economic exchange. Instead, Libya has maintained a schizophrenic relationship, in which it has constantly criticised and rejected its principal partner. At the same time, the rapprochement with Europe which has taken effect in recent years did not mean Gaddafi's African policy was to be abandoned. Libya had established an influence in the field of foreign policy and an economic presence in Africa which it was unwilling to forgo. On the contrary, Libya's objective is to be recognised within the Euro-Med Partnership as a major regional actor in the context of relations between the European Union and the African Union.

In addition, for the Libyan revolutionaries, the African continent is a "grey area" within which illicit cross-border traffic can be developed that will incidentally no doubt enrich the partisans of the African policy. Libyan investments in Africa are vast, and the returns from them are both enormous and not subjected to any form of scrutiny. Aside from the foreign policy issues raised by the African continent, Colonel Gaddafi is obliged to maintain a balance within Libya between the supporters of Europe and those of Africa. To sum up, for the reformers, Europe, and the West as a whole, represents an opportunity for the development of new and lucrative resources, while for the revolutionaries, the African continent is a certain and permanent source of income.

Conclusion

The new leaders of the organs of coercion, the new economic and diplomatic establishment, and tribesmen affiliated to the regime and to the family of Colonel Gaddafi, have all been instrumental in bringing about change within the regime. They have developed a novel rhetoric which has been brought to the attention of the international community by Gaddafi's heir apparent, Seif el-Islam. They have developed relationships of trust with the West in strategic fields such as oil and the war against terrorism. Finally they have constructed a new image of Libya, which is now definitively committed to expunge the memory of its revolutionary past, when Libya was linked to the idea of a terrorist State. Post-sanctions Libya has presented itself as the latest "Eldorado" for the West, this time within the Mediterranean region.

The conversion of the regime to its new "creed" has mobilised a range of networks within the State. In contrast to its Maghreb neighbours, the process of government in Libya has been subjected to little sociological study. While there is a substantial literature on the power of the army in Algeria, the Makhzen in Morocco, or the police state in Tunisia, the Libyan regime is customarily viewed solely in terms of its Head of State, Gaddafi himself. In reality, however, Gaddafi's hold on power is dependent on the existence of a range of networks within Libya, all lubricated by the country's oil wealth. The "conversion" of the regime has at last made it possible to look closely at its underlying sources of power. The basis on which the regime has deconstructed and reconstructed its system has become more evident in the light of the changes the regime has undergone.

The revolutionary regime has continuously dismantled and rebuilt itself over the course of four distinct periods, linked to successive crises. It has maintained its integrity throughout the periods of reform (1969-1973), crisis (1973-1977), revolution (1977-1989), and sanctions (1992-2003). The definitive raising of the sanctions has permitted the manner in which power has been concentrated in the hands of a restricted group of significant individuals to be clearly perceived. The collegiate aspect of the regime put in place by the Revolutionary Command Council developed into a circle which has comprised the most faithful companions of the Guide of the Revolution, together with those who have the most to gain from the maintenance of the system. The preceding chapter sought to show how the regime succeeded in profiting from the events of 11 September 2001, and from the Islamist threat which faces the international community. Since the appointment of a new government in 2003, the regime has constructed a new image for Libya. Through a kind of process of diplomatic seduction, the regime has been able to present an image of Libya as a new Eldorado, where an abundance of oil and the massive scale of the funds available for the modernisation of the infrastructure are an irresistible magnet for major international companies. In addition, post-sanctions Libya has definitively made the transition to a business-oriented State, and shares a vocabulary with the international community — "transparency", "the struggle against corruption" and even "democracy" — which firmly removes it from the list of "Terrorist States".

In 2003, the definitive removal of the sanctions was followed in Libya by a period of uncertainty as regards the future of the Jamahiriya, the political system identified with the revolutionary regime. The mechanisms which prevailed under the revolutionary regime, in the context of the "rentier State" included nationalist propaganda, the redistribution of wealth, the promotion of a "just society", and coercion. It might be hypothesised that these would take new forms in the context of the emergence of an authoritarian "mafia" regime. In such a regime the practices of an authoritarian state might coalesce with extra-legal methods of operation. Without its ideology of struggle, the regime took on the appearance of a "criminal enterprise", "capable of endowing itself with a territory, of taking control of vast economic resources, of controlling significant segments of local society and of imposing its will through the use of military force".[54]

These developments have been favoured by the grip exercised over Libya's oil resources by the members of the clans linked to the regime. Between 1993 and 1999, the effects of the international sanctions revealed the way the regime had closed ranks, relying on increasingly restricted governing circles. The sanctions showed that there were three centres of power, each of which was located within

a different structure. These were the security services, the National
Oil Corporation (NOC), and the Libyan Foreign Investment Company (LAFICO). These three organisations — representing security,
oil and financial interests — constituted the central core of the regime. The security services, which were the pillars of the regime,
guaranteed its survival. The NOC, one of the regime's most crucial
mechanisms, ensured financial continuity. The regime had very early
on released the NOC from all aspects of state control in order to give
it autonomy, so that oil production and exploitation were entirely
independent of the General People's Congress, though this remained
theoretically the supreme political body. LAFICO, the third centre
of power, was known as the "cassa forte" (the "strong box") by the
Italians. Though its headquarters were in modest offices in the centre
of Tripoli, its assets were distributed throughout a hundred countries
and a dozen offshore havens. American financial surveillance in the
1970s and 80s has disclosed in part the extent of LAFICO's holdings.
Given the indispensability of these three organisations to the regime,
it might be asked how possible it would be for the Jamahiriya to un-
dertake economic reforms. But will not the grip of the Gaddafis on
the oil revenue effectively condemn to failure all political and economic reform?

4

IS THE JAMAHIRIYA REFORMABLE?

The removal of international sanctions was followed by the promise of economic liberalisation in Libya. The regime sought to give itself an image attractive to foreign investors, especially in the energy, military and tourist sectors. In a sense, the regime was attempting to recover the appeal it had in the 1970s, when the image promoted by Libya was that of a "Mediterranean Emirate". Some saw the changes as a "return to the fold".[1] In practice, they took place because of the rise of new leaders shaped more by the world of business than by revolutionary ideology. New leaders have emerged within the regime's decision-making machinery, and in particular the coercive apparatus, who seek to commit Libya to globalisation. They wield influence across both the security and oil sectors, and have persuaded the Guide of the Revolution, Colonel Gaddafi, that Libya's "conversion" to globalisation would offer the most effective guarantee of the regime's continuation. They have taken encouragement from the observation that policies of liberalisation on the part of authoritarian Arab regimes had not led to changes in the political leadership — in fact quite the contrary.[2] They are gratified to have diverted the regime from a course leading it to inclusion in the "Axis of Evil". Now they seek to place Libya on the same footing as other authoritarian Arab regimes, specifically those in good standing with the international community thanks to their mastery of the standard vocabulary of globalisation.[3] Libya has clear advantages in this respect.

As part of putting this policy into action, the regime has given new status to the ministries, which have recovered a degree of authority they had lost. In key economic policy-making, however, the increasing power of technocratic decision makers has taken the place of ministerial authority. The ministries have no authority to make policy, and the decision-making process still lacks transparency. Between 1969 to 1999, Colonel Gaddafi strove to build a revolutionary State on the basis of the Basic Popular Committees. Politically, the role of the ministries was to provide the nascent revolutionary State with the organisational means to put policy into practice. In the absence of democratic political institutions, the "revolutionaries" — the members of the Basic People's Congress and the Revolutionary Committees —dictated to the ministries the policies which Gaddafi wished to implement. In practice the ministries themselves have long been the purview of technocrats: senior officials, able and well trained but with no political responsibility. The ministries enjoyed no autonomy in policy making, and their task was always to implement the revolutionary policy of the regime. Is this era at an end?

The appointment of Shukri Ghanem as Prime Minister on 14 June 2003 serves as an illustration of the growing power of the technocratic decision makers in the Libyan system. The Jamahiriya's deficiencies had resulted in the need to put it on a sounder financial and economic footing. The new government's goals — privatisation, liberalisation, reform and re-integration into the international community — required skills that the revolutionaries did not possess. For this reason, new leaders better grounded in economic ideas appeared within the ranks of the government. Shukri Ghanem's appointment to the position of Prime Minister indicated that trade and the economy were now the regime's first priorities. Other appointments in the same spirit were that of Abdelkader Belkhir to the Ministry of Economy and Commerce, Ammar Altaif to the new Ministry of Tourism and Fawzia

Shalabi to the Ministry of Culture. Further figures below the rank of minister who played a substantial role in the transition were Abdullah Salem al-Badri, the former Oil Minister; Abdulhafid Zlitni, ex-director of the NOC; Tarek Hassan Beek, the NOC's planning director; and Ahmed Abdulkarim, the head of OilInvest. The competencies of this group in the energy field lent credibility to the government's policies.

Another factor is that Libya's economic reorganisation is taking place an international climate highly conducive to its aims. The presence of the American troops in Iraq, and rising international oil prices, have both enhanced the comparative attractions offered by Libya. The appointment of a government which is both in touch and competent in regard to its oil policy has acted as a guarantee to foreign investors. The new Prime Minister appeared to be the right man to lead the process of reform. He had long served as Libya's representative at OPEC, where he had previously worked as a researcher, and held a doctorate in economics from Fletcher School of Law and Diplomacy at Tufts University. He was also the author of numerous studies of oil economics.[4] The ministerial reshuffle indicated a change of direction in Libya's political development, the previous government having failed either to attract international attention or to bring in foreign capital. Libya had been displaced from the focus of international attention by the Iraqi question, but returned with a vengeance in 2003 and embarked on a campaign to win the favour of the international community. The Libyans believed they had the resources with which to "whitewash" the regime. The case of the compensation for the families of the Lockerbie victims strengthened this view. The Libyan authorities have shown noteworthy pragmatism and an ability to seize their opportunities.

Libya: a Mediterranean Eldorado?

In contrast to the nightmare of Iraq, Libya is a dream for the oil companies. The overthrow of Saddam Hussein had held out the promise of access for the West to the world's second largest oil resources, as well as to substantial profits to be made by western companies in the reconstruction of a country reduced to the dark ages. Unexpectedly, however, it was Gaddafi's Libya that in fact emerged as the new Eldorado.[5] It should be said that in the post-sanctions period Libya exerted every effort to make itself more attractive to the major oil and industrial multinationals. In September 1999, the Minister for Planning and the Economy, Abdel Hafiz al-Zalaytani, said that between 2001 and 2005 the Libyan government planned to invest 35 billion dollars in its oil and electricity industries. 60 per cent of this was to be from State sources and 40 per cent direct inward investment from abroad. Over the coming 20 years, he said, the country would need investments totalling some 150 billion dollars, of which 60 per cent would be provided by the State. Libya's plans were vast, but not out of proportion to its financial resources. In contrast to Iraq, Libya was solvent and free of risk. All these were important factors for the Libyan government, of which it needed to make use in the context of its re-positioning on the "good" side.

Libyan blandishments

In 2003, Ahmed Abdulkarim, the former chairman of the NOC and the current head of OilInvest, announced that in the field of oil and gas alone the government was looking to attract 10 billion dollars of foreign investment before 2010. Only 25 per cent of the reserves of oil and gas, currently estimated at 40 billion barrels, are under exploitation. In 2004, Libya produced around 1.5 million barrels per day (bpd), but the government's aim is to increase production to 1.8 million bpd in 2006 and 3 million bpd by 2020. This would restore production to the level it had reached before 1970, when Libya produced 3.3 bpd. Libya has greatly improved the terms under which foreign firms invest in the energy sector. In 1996, the Energy Minister, Abdullah al-Badri, announced that Law 25 of 1955 on oil exploitation required amendment, in order to bring the Libyan market into line with the needs of the international oil industry. In 1998, a preparatory committee under the chairmanship of Mohammed al-Kaylani, a senior official in the Energy industry, produced a draft document setting out the basis for new oil legislation.[6] In addition, in April 1999, just two weeks after the suspension of the sanctions, the Energy Minister, Abdullah al-Badri, confirmed that Libya had made a commitment to open its energy sector to as many international companies as possible, noting that there were 96 separate blocs of territory available for exploitation.[7]

As well as investment in the oil sector, Libya is also in need of investment in the urban infrastructure. After the suspension of the sanctions in April 1999, the Libyan government embarked on an ambitious plan of investment in many sectors. With the national currency now on a sound footing, the Libyans has hopes that direct foreign investment in non-oil sectors will rapidly be resumed. Transport and tourism are prime targets. Libyan Arab Airlines had already declared its intention to renew its fleet, which had been badly affected by the embargo on air transport. Its requirements total nine billion dollars, which would include the purchase of aircraft, pilot training, and the refurbishment of airports. The Libyan government has also indicated its interest in the construction of a railway line along the coast, on the grounds that trade with neighbouring countries was on the increase. The percentages of Libya's total exports and imports which relate to neighbouring states have risen to 11 per cent for Tunisia, 8 per cent for Egypt, 6 per cent for Morocco and 10 per cent for Sudan. Finally, it is in the tourism sector that Libya's desire to liberalise its market is most evident. In April 2000, the International Fair in Tripoli illustrated the interest of European businesses in the Libyan market. Beyond the immediate needs of the government, Libya has its attractions in other sectors, including in particular the resumption of arms imports, as well as the supply and distribution of water. In the field of infrastructure, the government launched a range of projects. The Socialist Port Authority, which controls the seven commercial ports, envisages the expansion of the port of Misurata to cope with an annual total of six million tonnes of goods. The Railway Executive Board has a scheme for a railway network including a line of 600 kilometres from Sirte to Benghazi and a 470-kilometre line from Benghazi to Tobruk, and a Metro line in Tripoli is under consideration. All these economic plans have attracted the attention of foreign investors, and have changed the image of Libya. From a "Terrorist State", Libya has transformed itself into a leading market.

Surprisingly, the arms sector has attracted the keenest competition. For example, Putin's Russia is ambitious to re-enter the Libyan arms market, which had formerly been a good opportunity for the Soviet Union, and which — like the oil sector — is now wide open.[8] In 2004, Libya once more became a potential customer for the international arms trade. In this area too, its requirements were enormous. Having forsworn WMD, Libya's goal is to reconstruct its conventional military power. With this demand in view, the arms industries of Russia, Britain, Germany, Italy and France were in competition.[9] But how could the resumption of arms sales to Libya be justified? In the 1970s and 1980s, Libya's indiscriminate arms purchases led it into the series of conflicts which culminated in the international sanctions. Libya's arms expenditure totalled 28 billion dollars between 1973 and 1983. The lifting of the United Nations sanctions did not in itself permit the resumption of arms exports to Libya, since there was also a European Union ban on arms sales. Not until October 2004 was the European Union able to remove its ban, even then raising some concerns. The lifting of the European Union sanctions revealed a certain degree of reluctance. On 22 October 2004, in a debate at the Western European Union, a British representative, Lord Russell-Johnston, said: "No sooner does Libya begin to behave better than the first reaction of the European Union is to sell it arms.... This is not the best solution." The question for Libya was how to persuade international opinion — if this were to prove necessary — that Libya had a real need to resume its conventional armaments policy.

The argument for the lifting of the European Union sanctions on arms sales ban would in the end be based on the need to provide Libya with the means to combat illegal migration.[10] In September 2004, a month before the EU decision, Italy gave a clear signal that it wished to assist the Libyan regime to acquire the range of military equipment needed to control the movements of migrants, including new radar equipment, helicopters, optical surveillance equipment and patrol boats. On the grounds that an "invasion" of African migrants was arriving from Libya, which had already resulted in the illegal residence in Italy of some two million Africans, Italy persuaded its European partners to lift the ban on arms sales to Libya. In return, Libya would authorise the establishment on Libyan soil of reception centres for clandestine migrants. The instrumentalisation of the issue of migration for military and commercial purposes had the desired effect. The proposal was accepted, and the European Union lifted the ban on arms sales to Libya.

Thus, in practice, Libya succeeded in making the case that it represented an Eldorado for the oil companies and a leading market for the arms industry, at precisely the moment when the Middle East market had become saturated. The projection of this new image and Europe's belief in Libya's metamorphosis strengthened the conviction of the Libyan authorities that Europe operated only on the basis of interests, and not on principles. Visits by European political leaders to Tripoli strengthened the conviction of the Libyan government that it had "triumphed" over the sanctions. According to the Libyan news agency Jana, in a report dated 11 October 2004, immediately after the lifting of the ban on arms sales to Libya: "Libya is one of the first countries to dismantle its WMD programme voluntarily under international supervision.... This policy is a further major political triumph, which is a demonstration of the strength of will of the Great Jamahiriya, thanks to the steadfastness of its people and its determination never to surrender.... This victory demonstrates the failure of the policy of sanctions, boycott and blockade."

The curse of oil?

Once it had resumed its place in the international community, the Libyan regime opened its economy to foreign investors. Reforms were also promised, prompting the question whether this signalled the end of the "Rentier State". Libya's economy was entirely based on the sale of oil, and was therefore at the mercy of oil prices. In addition, it was neither controlled by the laws of supply and demand, nor was it planned, but was subject to the "directives" of the Guide, who had his own clear ideas about the economy. In January 2000, in his speech to the General People's Congress, he outlined his recent thinking on the economy and the sectors in which the government should be investing. He slammed the administration for its failure to use computer resources: "The entire world uses computers for administration and management, while you still insist on spending 100 per cent of our oil income on salaries. We no longer want people to waste their time producing documents, certificates and affidavits. All information should be on little cards with silicon chips. You put the card in the computer and all the information and details appear on the screen.... You stick to outdated ways as an excuse for wasting oil. Oil should be for building and for infrastructure: ports, airports, roads, water supplies, reservoirs, and all those indispensable things we could not have without oil, such as health and education. Oil should buy us missiles, submarines, combat aircraft. Our industry and agriculture should make us self-sufficient, and even — why not? — be exported to earn foreign currency."[11] All this was prompted by Gaddafi's awareness that Libya, despite its oil wealth, was a poor country, under-equipped and chaotic in its organisation. Michael L. Ross's conjecture seems well founded: "There is now strong evidence that states with abundant resource wealth perform less than their resource-poor counterparts."[12] The deleterious effects of the oil income were to be seen in the spread of corruption.

Transparency International, in its index of the perception of corruption in 2003, ranked Libya in 118th place out of 133 states surveyed. For this reason, the Michigan District Export Council earnestly recommended in its guide for businessmen that they should be wary when operating in Libya: "Beware of middlemen. Libya has seen a proliferation of unscrupulous "western" and Libyan agencies claiming to be able to arrange with specific, high-profile individuals. Go through the front door. Do not attempt to circumvent bidding processes by finding special sources of patronage or going through a local middleman."[13] Actually, the ubiquity of middlemen in commercial transaction results from the lack of transparency of the regime. Middlemen present themselves as essential elements in the attempt to reach decision-makers. After all, who decides what in Libya?

The nature of the Libyan political system means that intermediaries are indispensable. Their role is a necessary one due to the arbitrary nature of policy making and the lack of transparency in the decision-making process. Foreign governments establish direct links with members of Gaddafi's family — usually his children or cousins — in order to initiate new programmes of cooperation or to resolve disputes, should the need arise, or to put in place new means of cooperation. Major foreign companies have attempted to follow the example of government in setting up similar links. However, only a very few enjoy direct access to the family like that of the Italian company Fiat, which has Saadi, one of Gaddafi's sons, as a member of its administrative council.

In addition to the concentration of political power in the hands of a restricted number of decision-makers, the nation's wealth is exclusively controlled, without any accountability by a relatively small number of people. In this way, the State's resources are diverted to projects of Pharaonic proportions at the sole instance of Gaddafi and his close circle of policy-makers. An example is the Great Underground River, whose cost is put at 40 billion dollars; another was the arms purchasing policy of the 1980s, estimated to have cost 28 billion dollars. No political institution is empowered to scrutinise the use of State resources, the officials who carry out transactions, or the sums involved. The magazine *Jeune Afrique*, in a report whose facts are hard to verify, has calculated that between 1973 and 2003, more than 360 billion dollars passed through the hands of the regime.[14] The journalist investigated what the money was used for, and how much of it remains. It seems likely that the costs of the Great Underground River and the arms purchases absorbed a portion of this sum. Infrastructure investment and current costs account for another part of the oil income. Many questions remain unanswered concerning the elite's wealth and its holdings in overseas companies and investments in offshore funds. In the view of Transparency International, Libya is a country where corruption has reached alarming levels.

At the same time, a legal mechanism exists which is intended to combat corruption. On 10 October 1999, at a conference in Durban on anti-corruption measures, Abdurrahman Musa al-Abbar, the secretary-general of the Popular Committee at the Council for Popular Control, gave an account of the measures Libya has taken against corruption. According to the Libyan official these included: "Law number 2 of 1979, concerning economic crimes, which is related to fighting all aspects of economic corruption in the state. Law number 6 of 1985 regarding prohibition of favouritism; and law number 3 of 1986 required the disclosure of the origin of assets, in a measure relating to the prohibition of improper gains. Law Number 10 of year 1994 regarding purification. This was enacted to fight all kinds of corruption in the community. This law compels all general employees and self-employed citizens to submit annual declarations on their financial positions and the extent of their modification during the period covered by the declaration."[15] But what is really happening in terms of corruption in Libya? The perception of a "level of corruption" says little about corruption in practice or what form it takes. In reality, corruption forms part of a process of interaction which is not perceived by the Libyan leadership as reprehensible, given that the concept of public assets is not well developed.

For instance, despite the formal existence of controls, scrutiny of public expenditure remains arbitrary. The distribution of oil wealth is unsupervised by any public authority and takes the form of goods and services. Good, services, and basic products — for example, education, health, housing, transport — are available to the population because they are subsidised by the regime. The Libyan people have a relatively high standard of living in relation to other countries in the region. However, the process of distribution is arbitrary, and can at any moment be halted. The redistributive function of the Jamahiriya is crucial. From it, Colonel Gaddafi in part derives his legitimacy. In 1996, Gaddafi personally distributed 5000 dollars to 300,000 families, to help them cope with the difficulties due to the sanctions. He took this money from the Oil Fund Reserve, a financial organ over which no control is exercised, which amounted in 2002 to 8.8 billion dollars.[16] All Libyan opposition parties have condemned the regime's corruption. The largest of these, the National Front for the Salvation of Libya, says control over State finances is crucial, and has referred to "calls by many Libyan opposition groups, urging and highlighting the need to consolidate the appropriate resources in a way that would best serve the Libyan issue."[17] The dissipation of Libya's oil resources by Gaddafi is a criticism often voiced. Gaddafi's generosity towards various African Heads of State is legendary. For example, the leaders of South Africa and Ghana were each presented with a Mercedes S500, at a cost of 100,000 dollars per car, while another former president allegedly received cash payments delivered in a suitcase. The Libyan Arab African Investment Company (LAAICO) has invested four billion dollars in Africa, with more than 130 projects brought to fruition, and owns outright a number of industrial enterprises in such countries as Ghana, Gabon, Liberia, Zambia and Congo Brazzaville.[18] Mohammed Elhuweij, Gaddafi's banker, who was Minister of Finance in the government of Shukri Ghanem, was previously head of the Council for Foreign Investments. In the context of the prevailing economic crisis, the Libyan people were surprised by the extent of Libya's investment in Africa, while Libya itself had many needs.

Corruption in the Libya political system is inherent in the nature of the regime. The absence of political and civil liberties has left the decision makers in unchallenged control of public resources. The utilisation of these resources takes place without any safeguards and often in pursuit of objectives which have little to do with popular expectations. As the regime sees it, the nation's wealth was there to promote the realisation of the "revolutionary project". Fundamentally, the use of public resources for personal or political ends relates to a wider problem: that of the status of the State within Arab society. The government of a State is perceived — according to the anthropologist Michel Seurat — as a "'common sensibility' [asabiyya] which has succeeded".[19] The State is not seen as a political instrument at the service of the collectivity and the public good, but as a power at the service of a tribe which has obtained for itself control of the State's mechanisms.

The extreme concentration of power in the hands of a small group of policy makers, who are responsible to no-one, provides latitude for corrupt practices. However, the Libyan policy makers do not share the ill-repute of the "Algerian generals" who take a percentage on all contracts. Corruption in Libya is subtler, and furthermore is not always perceived by Libyans as a morally and commercially reprehensible practice. Libyan policy makers regard foreign operators as guests, whom they have allowed to take part in an interaction whose value goes beyond its strictly commercial or economic limits. The conclusion of a contract may be the culmination of a family relationship or one of friendship — as is the case with Italian investors — that is honoured by the clinching of a deal that is privileged inasmuch as it implies the exclusion of other participants. The oil sector is seen as the decision makers' particular fief, which they share with "guests" whom they have chosen for diplomatic, military or political reasons, or out of considerations of friendship. Overtly, they demand no entry fee, but they do recommend international companies which operate in Libya to cooperate with their own companies. As they see it, this is an above-board exchange, which has nothing to do with corruption. The oil and gas sector is very sequestered, employing 35,000 people who are kept under close surveillance by the Revolutionary Committees. The almost exclusive control exercised by the Gaddafi family and those policy makers who enjoy the Guide's trust would render any attempt at corruption both very uncertain and extremely risky. The oil and gas sector is the object of particular attention on the part of the regime: it is both the property of a single family and the driving force of Libya's redistributive State. In this light, such corruption as exists in the oil sector is very oblique and takes place at the level of the control and management of hydrocarbon sales.

On the other hand, corruption in the banking sector takes place on a significant scale. Inter alia, this takes the form of speculation over exchange rates, the feeding of the unofficial currency market, or a lack of transparency over the quantities of currency exchanged. Though the harmonisation of rates of exchange and the emergence of a private banking sector have considerably reduced the speculation in foreign currency, it does continue. Two private banks have opened: the Bank of Commerce and Development (BCD), and the National Banking Corporation.[20] Following the pattern of the oil sector, the advocates of privatisation have persuaded Libya's decision makers to liberalise the banking sector. At the moment, these two banks provide credit for the purchase of consumer goods, and look likely to increase the loans they offer in the fields of chemical industry, factories and assembly plants. The sectors of pharmacy and telecommunications, which for the moment work only with the National Commerce Bank, are also expected to accept private credit. On the other hand, the National Oil Corporation, which currently deals exclusively with the Central Bank and with the Libyan Arab Foreign Bank, does not seem to be involved in such exercises in liberalisation. The liberalisation of the Libyan economy exposes the nature of its "governance" to foreign participants, who do not fail to point out certain elementary conventions in the management of public affairs.

Necessary but impossible reforms

In August 2003, a group of members of the executive board of the IMF undertook a high level consultancy mission to Libya. The recommendations of the IMF, were they to be applied, could not fail to lead to greater transparency: "They urged the authorities to implement stricter control over all extra-budgetary funds, particularly the Oil Reserve Fund, and reassess the mechanical distribution of oil revenue between capital and current expenditures.... They urged the authorities to move toward greater budget transparency and to cast the budget within a coordinated medium-term framework that takes into account the non-renewable nature of Libya's hydrocarbon resources."[21] One of the major challenges in the struggle against corruption in Libya is to institute a method of accounting publicly for the State's resources. The absence of any underlying means to allow an objective evaluation of the government's income tends to set the scene for corrupt practices. The IMF made the following recommendation to Libya: "Directors welcomed the improvements in Libya's statistical database. They emphasized, however, that its further strengthening should be accorded a high priority. They encouraged the authorities to participate in the Fund's general data Dissemination System." Following the termination of the sanctions, the Libyan authorities sent encouraging signals that the economic structure of the Jamahiriya would undergo fundamental changes. Libya made a formal demand for advice from the World Bank, with the purpose of assisting it to become part of the global economy. Gaddafi's aim was to prepare Libya for membership of the World Trade Organisation (WTO). In response, the World Bank was to produce its first report on Libya since 1958.

The challenge of achieving transparency was daunting. The upheavals taking place would have been quite simply unimaginable in 2000. In the short term, the primary objective of economic liberalisation is to satisfy the demands of a society which had become frustrated in the course of a decade of sanctions. The Jamahiriya's economic and political decline has given rise to popular dissatisfaction. The regime's only option for the satisfaction of popular expectations is to prepare the way for the emergence of a consumer society. Economic liberalisation, however, does not mean political freedom. Libya's liberalisation is more in the style of China's "communist capitalism" than that of the Soviet Union's perestroika. Libya's political structures remain unaltered, so that it is hard to see how there could be major progress in the struggle against corruption. This is all the more difficult as any such move would arouse the resentment — or the outright hostility — of the "revolutionaries", who feared the opening of such a Pandora's box.[22] From the point of view of those who serve it, the Jamahiriya is a powerful instrument for personal enrichment, which operates under the cloak of a profound lack of transparency. Any questions raised about such an economic system will cause unease. But how otherwise can the promise of economic reform be made credible?

Nevertheless, substantial change has been achieved. The Gaddafi regime is aware of its credibility deficit, and of the high level of suspicion felt by foreign businesses. The reforms initiated by the Shukri Ghanem government are part of a broader policy intended to present Libya as attractive and credible to foreign investors. The need to modernise or even renew Libya's economic and oil infrastructure has obliged the Libyan government to place oil exploitation on a competitive and stable footing. Economic liberalisation is a response to favourable international and economic circumstances. For the moment, however, there is no reason to believe that liberalisation will inaugurate any process intended to bring about deeper reform of the Libyan economy, or, to be more precise, to bring transparency to the handling of Libya's oil income.

A further issue is that liberalisation intended to favour foreign investors has gone hand in hand with discussion of the privatisation of national enterprises, as well as encouragement for the establishment of private businesses.[23] In June 2000, Ammar Eltief, (the President of the National Institute for Information and Documentation) set out the priorities: "The issue is to put the ownership of large enterprises back in the hands of the Libyan people. The proposed law provides that no single person shall own a large number of shares, to avoid concentration in a few hands. I repeat that this will be a 'horizontal' privatisation, and that we do not intend to embark on the road of capitalism. What is at issue is the restitution of property: what belongs to the people should return to the people. At the centre of our concerns — which relate not only to economics but also to demography — lies the arrival of an entire new cohort of young working Libyans on to the labour market, where there are already a million foreign workers. The difficulty with Libyans is that they are very fussy about their choice of jobs."[24] But how can an oil state be reformed? Up to now, reform has consisted of promoting greater autonomy at the local level.

The policy of decentralisation,[25] which has enabled local collectivities to exercise an autonomous economic policy, is aimed to promote economic initiatives at the local level. Amongst other activities, local authorities have been authorised to issue import and export licenses, and to set and run their own budgets. From 1999, provinces and municipalities were given autonomy from the central authorities. Local governments were not obliged to seek ministerial authorisation to institute policies at the local level in investment, job creation and construction. It must be said that the degree of economic liberalisation so far achieved remains very limited, due to the reluctance of foreign investors. The regime's lack of transparency, the arbitrary nature of policy making, and the image of a "corrupt State" have been the obstacles to economic liberalisation. Aware of this negative image,[26] the government has put transparency at the top of its priorities. But the country's oil income is more a political tool than an economic resource. Libya's economic policy since the 1970s has shown with great clarity that the first priority of the regime has been political and ideological problems, at the expense of a strategy for economic modernisation.

The foreign policy uses of oil income

Oil income has been great enough to fund the construction of an authoritarian regime, as well as support for terrorism, the acquisition of a substantial arsenal of weapons, and finally the payment of compensation to the victims of terrorist attacks. How effective has its use been, however, in the development of the oil industry or the modernisation of the economic infrastructure? The economic dimension has in fact been very largely neglected, in preference to activities which the regime has deemed more important, such as support for terrorism and the development of an interdependent relationship with Europe. Libya's economic deficiencies, it should be said, are only partial, and resulting from the regime's other preoccupations.These are oriented towards its political and foreign policy goals.

The foreign policy developed by the regime is based on oil. Under the sanctions, European companies received pressing invitations to operate in Libya. Once the sanctions were lifted, the American companies were given privileged treatment. The regime was aware of the influence of oil lobbyists in the western democracies, and set up a special task force to present a credible image of Libya's policy of liberalisation in the hydrocarbon sector. The policy of persuasion directed at the American companies indicates the central role of the National Oil Corporation (NOC) in the machinery of Libya's oil-based foreign policy. Analysis of the NOC's activities also demonstrates the intimate linkage between the oil sector and the security functions of the State.

The lifting of the sanctions changed Libya's priorities. Up to then, the European oil companies had served as a bulwark against any hypothetical strengthening of the embargo that might be demanded by the Clinton administration. Now, however, the international oil companies came to represent, in Libya's eyes, a major channel through which their respective governments might be persuaded to accept Libya's return to the international scene. In this context, the American and British companies were especially important. For example, well in advance of 11 September 2000, Ahmed Abdulkarim, a leading figure in the NOC, opened negotiations with Marathon, Amerada Hess, Conoco and Oxy over Libya's rehabilitation.[27] Following 11 September 2001, Libya at once became more amenable to the political and security demands of the United States. These included the payment of compensation to the families of victims, the dismissal of more than 130 Libyan officials suspected of implication in terrorism, the cessation of Libyan involvement in the Palestinian issue, and a halt to the development of WMD.[28] All this was traceable to the fear that Libya might share the fate of Saddam Hussein's Iraq. Libya initially sought the return of the American oil companies under the same terms as before and then facilitated further investment. Libya's short term goal was to distance itself from the "Axis of Evil" and to be dropped from the list of rogue states. Libya had the benefit of a favourable climate in the United States. The influential think-tank, the Atlantic Council, with the sponsorship of the American oil companies, had already produced a report on the benefits of an American return to Libya, under the title "US-Libyan Relations: Towards Cautious Re-engagement".

The return of the American oil companies

The promotion of the return of the American oil companies was one of the primary objectives of the government of Shukri Ghanem. In its pursuit, he sought to accelerate a process that had begun in May 2000. The previous government had opened "137 blocks" to be negotiated as new concessions. The Libyan government wanted to persuade the international companies to step up the level of their participation in oil exploration and exploitation, especially in the Murzuq Basin in the south-west of the country. The Spanish company Repsol had discovered significant oil reserves in the area. The development of Murzuq, had been under the control of the NOC since November 2000. The NOC had invited foreign companies to participate, but only five Blocks had been assigned. The NOC was also involved in the exploitation of the Sirte Basin, and Ghadames.

A further goal was the promotion of exploration in the unexploited parts of Kufra and Cyrenaica.[29] Shukri Ghanem announced that Libya intended to auction 39 Blocks where oil had been discovered but not commercialised. The international companies felt that so far the process of assigning concessions had been dilatory. Negotiations had gone further with European companies such as Repsol and ENI, which had already considerably increased their presence in Libya during the sanctions era.

In September 2004, however in an unusual move, Shukri Ghanem's government put up for auction the exploration rights of 15 offshore and onshore zones.[30] This procedure was intended to be the most transparent method of selecting foreign collaborators. The government promised that the process would be transparent, and would represent a break with the murky and arbitrary proceedings that had so far characterised Libyan decision making. This novel procedure was supposed to demonstrate the new authority of the Shukri Ghanem government over the complex decision making process. The Prime Minister had succeeded in convincing Gaddafi's unofficial immediate circles that Libya must alter its attitude if it wanted to persuade foreign investors to return. The new government thus demonstrated that the modernisation of Libya's economy and infrastructure had to be accompanied by changes in commercial practices. The shortcomings of the previous government were traceable in part to the inability of the former Prime Minister, Mubarak el-Shamekh, to make a credible case for the liberalisation of Libya's economy, especially in the sphere of oil. The slowness of decision-making — which was due to intense behind-the-scenes negotiation — was in part responsible for foreign investors' disenchantment over the reality of liberalisation in Libya. In this context, an analysis of EPSA 4 — the latest version of the Exploration and Production Sharing Agreement, covering the auction of concessions — is revealing for the information it provides about changes inside Libya.

EPSA IV

The Libyan authorities had allotted the existing concession contracts to foreign operators within the framework of the original EPSA agreement, which had been effective from 1974. EPSA 1 allowed Exxon, Mobil, Total, Elf Aquitaine, Braspetro and Agip to participate in production. In 1980, the agreement was revised. EPSA 2, though on less attractive terms, permitted further companies to take part. These were Occidental, Oasis Consortium, Shell, Deminex, Veba Oel, Wintershall, Rompetrol and Geocom. In 1988, the departure of the American companies, following the diplomatic crisis, obliged Libya to revise the framework of the agreement in order to make up for the absence of the companies. EPSA 3 gave foreign companies better conditions. The companies were invited to operate within the framework of joint ventures with the NOC, which should hold at least 51 per cent of any joint venture. The allocation of production was 25 per cent for the foreign company and 75 per cent for the NOC, with the foreign company bearing 100 per cent of exploration costs and 50 per cent of investment in production. Between 1988 and 1995, more than 25 foreign oil companies became involved Libya's hydrocarbon sector.[31] For EPSA 4, the procedure was as follows:

Invitation to bid — Round 1:[32]

"All interested companies are invited to a presentation on contractual framework, a technical summary of the individual areas and a Bidding Process terms and conditions for this first bid round followed by discussion. The dates, venues and times are as follows :

5/9/2004, Tripoli at the Mehari Hotel at 10:00 a.m.

14/9/2004, London at Hilton Langham Hotel at 10:00 a.m.

All companies, individually or consortiums, interested to participate in the Bidding Process shall be required to address an Application Letter to NOC and submit certain qualification documentations not later than 28/9/2004. NOC will study and evaluate all Applications according to its Guidelines and Procedures for Public Bidding and will deliver its decision, in writing, to all qualified companies/consortiums (the "Bidders") not later than 19/10/2004, applicants currently operating in Libya are exempted from the qualification requirements.

A Data Room session will be held in Tripoli at NOC premises during the period 20/10/2004 until 29/10/2004. Qualified Bidders only will have access to the Data Room. During the Data Room session, Bidder will receive, for each area its interest, a complete Bid Package containing: instructions and Bidding procedures; technical data; the EPSA model; Commitment Letter; Form of Bid Guaranty. Data Room fee is charged, as specified above, and required to be paid prior to visiting the Data Room.

Bidders may request a clarification meeting during the period 6/11/2004 to 24/11/2004, the purpose of which shall be to clarify any enquiries and comments that they may have. NOC may accept certain comments, in which case, NOC will include these in the Bidding Package as relevant and will circulate same to all Bidders before 3/12/2004.

Bidders are required to submit their Bids in a sealed envelope, delivered by hand, between 08:00 am and 10:00 am on 10/1/2005 (the "Bid Opening Date) at the Mehari hotel in Tripoli. A bid opening ceremony will be conducted in public and in the presence of the legal representatives of the Bidders on the Bid Opening Date. Except for a single Bidder or in case of a draw, the winning Bidder wil be announced at the end of the session.

Bidders are also required to submit, on the Bid Opening date, a Bid Guaranty issued by the Libyan Arab Foreign Bank. Guaranty Form and other related details are available in the Bid Package. Except for the winning Bidder and Sole bidder, if any, Bid Guaranties will be returned to Bidders".

Area Bassin	Blocks	Acreage.km2	Data room fees, US dollars
018-offshore	4	10307	30,725
035-offshore	4	9070	12,510
036-offshore	4	10414	12,750
047-offshore	4	6182	32,595
052-offshore	4	8047	19,290
053-offshore	4	9769	22,940
054-offshore	4	10531	18,780
059-Cyrénaica	2	5298	15,450
065-Ghadames	2	4374	61,880
086-Sirte	4	7087	19,070
106-Sirte	4	6520	129,565
124-Sirte	3	6113	67,380
131-Murzuk	4	10381	29,140
163-Murzuk	4	11236	43,865
177-Murzuk	4	11317	36,880

The concessions allocated under EPSA 4 displayed the extent to which the oil sector was a foreign policy instrument for Libya. American companies obtained nine Blocks out of the 15 on offer.[33] The political and foreign policy objective was achieved: the American companies had returned, thanks to the liberalisation of the hydrocarbon sector.

Non-official organisations sprang up to control the process of distributing the funds and assigning the expenses involved in this "bonanza". The maintenance of the power of Gaddafi's family and his tribal relatives depended on their ability to control the access to oil. The nationalisation of oil and gas resources in the 1970s, followed by the controlled opening up of access, had given them complete domination over energy resources and a substantial increase in their income. For this reason, the liberalisation of the oil sector, in the view of ruling circles in Libya, should not become a kind of perestroika, that could lead inexorably onward to the legitimacy of the government being called into question. A parallel phenomenon would be the way in which Algeria's liberalisation in the late 1980s led to the destabilisation of the FLN state.[34] Unchallenged control of the oil income was a political imperative for the continuation of the regime. To this end, the regime needed to modernise and transform the industry's ageing infrastructure. The regime therefore appealed for foreign companies to invest, which it saw as the only way, in current circumstances, of achieving this objective. The installation of a government with expertise in the oil sector was a powerful signal to the international companies. This government was primarily entrusted with the task of paving the way for the return of the American oil companies. The return of the Oasis Group (Amerada Hess, Conoco, Grace Petroleum), which had left Libya in 1986 following Ronald Reagan's ruling that all relations must be broken off with Libya, was an important goal. The hope was that a powerful lobby would thus be created that would be capable of putting pressure on the Bush administration to remove Libya from the list of terrorist states. The Oasis Group had in any case

been engaged for some months in negotiations for the return of the 41
per cent share it had previously held in the Waha Oil Field.[35]

For foreign policy, military and political reasons, therefore, the
Shukri Ghanem government needed to satisfy the demands of the
American oil companies. More or less secret negotiations had taken
place in recent years in which undertakings had been made both by
Libya and by the British and Americans. Libya had agreed among
other things to compensate the families of victims, halt its WMD programme and help in the struggle against terrorism, while the British
and Americans committed themselves to drop any legal proceedings
against Colonel Gaddafi, re-establish diplomatic relations and reopen
military cooperation.[36] In parallel, commercial negotiations were held
with the Oasis Group (composed of Amerada Hess, Conoco, Grace
Petroleum) which had quit Libya in 1986 following President Reagan's
order to break off all relations. The Libyan government hoped this
would result in the return of the major oil companies, such as Exxon
and Mobil, which had left Libya in 1982. A further 40 exploitation
licenses were auctioned in March 2005. The merged ExxonMobil, on
the principle that Libya was a country it could not afford to ignore,
in fact returned to Libya in December 2005 with a deal involving the
NOC.[37] The Oasis Group's concessions, which had been taken over
by the Waha Oil Company, and which were due to expire in 2005,
were restored as a gesture of Libya's good faith. Overall, the Libyan
government's objective is to rebuild a relationship of confidence between the regime and the American and British governments. What
lay behind the privileged treatment given to the British and American
companies in Libya was the regime's objective of the restoration of
diplomatic ties, which has of course now been achieved. As time went
on, the Libyan government was fundamentally shifting its position. Oil
is a highly sensitive issue, because of its strategic dimension, and real
influence is the prerogative of only a very few figures, drawn largely
either from the sphere of Gaddafi's family, or from among the senior
officials of the oil industry. The influence of the latter varies with the

prevailing international circumstances. In the 1970s and 1980s, the leading figures of the oil sector had been highly influential.[38] Later, however, because of the changing policies of the regime, the faction in the ascendant was that of the "liberalisers", whose principal objective was the return of the British and American oil companies.

In this context, the historic visit to Tripoli by Tony Blair in May 2003 was the culmination of a series of prior accords on foreign policy and military issues. Carried away by the euphoria of their diplomatic coup, the Libyans went as far in 2003 as to propose the possibility of a summit in Madrid in which Gaddafi would participate together with the then Spanish Prime Minister José Aznar, Tony Blair and President Bush. Gaddafi's heir apparent, Seif el-Islam, believed that the international system had been overturned by the 11 September 2001 attacks, and joined the government in its efforts to bring Libya into the "good camp" — the allies of the United States. Libya has much to offer which could not fail to interest its new allies. In addition to its oil, it has its anti-terrorist experience, together with a strategic depth in Africa which would be of help with ExxonMobil's commitments in Chad and Sudan. Libya's preference for the Anglo-Saxon companies is systematic. In March 2004, the British organised a mission to Libya, involving "UK Trade and Investment" as well as the "Energy Industries Council", whose remit was to develop British understanding of Libya's "business culture". The large number of companies that took part was an indication Britain's anxiety to discover whether Libya had the ability to set up a manufacturing industry. Libya's industry would not in its current state have been able to supply the demand for products that would result from foreign participation in the energy sector. The agreement between Blair and Gaddafi on training for the Libyan army was also a factor in the allocation by the Libyan authorities of licenses to foreign operators in the oil industry. President Chirac's visit to Tripoli in November 2004, followed by that of the French Minister of Defence, were part of a similar process: that of promising military cooperation in exchange for a better deal for the French oil companies in Libya.

There was a clear linkage between access to the Libyan oil market and the warmth or otherwise of the relations between Libya and the various countries involved. For instance, the exploration licences which were allocated in 2003 to the Spanish company Repsol and the Austrian OMV Group in the allocation of licenses in 2000 by the Libyan NOC amounted to a form of reward for those European companies which had assisted Libya under the sanctions. The maintenance of Libyan production during the sanctions was achieved in large part as the result of the continued participation of European companies such as Repsol, OMV, Agip, Wintershall and Total.[39] The good relations between Joerg Haider's Austria, and certain other European political figures led to rumours of clandestine Libyan support for certain European political parties. Similarly, immediately after the suspension of the sanctions in April 1999, the strong encouragement of French investment by the Libyan authorities was a reward for France's role in promoting Libya's case at the United Nations. However, when France threatened that it might withhold its vote for the definitive raising of the sanctions if Libya failed to compensate the families of the French victims at the level demanded, commercial negotiations in Libya were frozen, to the disadvantage of the French companies involved.

Strengthening relations with Europe

Libya exports 90 per cent of its oil to Europe.[40] Oil was a diplomatic weapon for Libya during the sanctions period, from 1992 to 1999. Libya's priority was to maintain its oil production despite the sanctions. The few foreign companies that showed an interest in oil production were encouraged to participate. The strategic partnership between Libya and Italy tended to work in favour of the Italian companies, which had excellent relations with Libya. Germany and Switzerland also developed a partnership with Libya which helped their oil companies to become established.[41] Similarly, the Spanish company Repsol took a high profile in Libya during the sanctions. The presence of the European oil companies under the sanctions was a considerable help to Libya in mitigating the intensity of its conflictual relationship with the United States. Actually, the Clinton administration did consider the option of toughening the sanctions against Libya by including the oil industry in their scope. In practice, a gamut of sanctions was brought to bear to penalise foreign companies which invested in Libya. Italy and Germany indicated clearly to the United States their opposition to sanctions on Libya, on the grounds of Libya's key position as an oil supplier. The proportion of Libya's oil which was exported to Europe was massive. In 1999, 974,000 barrels per day (bpd) went to Europe out a total production of 991,000 bpd. Italy and Germany imported respectively 438,000 bpd and 250,000 bpd, representing together around 70 per cent of Libya's production.[42]

The development of an interdependent relationship with Europe in the field of energy supplies was a considerable boost to Libya in foreign policy terms during the period of tension with the United States. The Italian company Agip had operated in Libya since the 1960s, and was the leading oil producer. Agip had survived all the various phases which had marked the Jamahiriya's trajectory, from the first oil discoveries in 1959 up to the definitive lifting of sanctions in September 2003. Following the nationalisation in the early 1970s, exploration agreements were reached within the framework of EPSA 1. These allowed such companies as Elf Aquitaine, Agip, the Brazilian-owned company Braspetro, Exxon, Mobil, Total and the Indian company ONGC to continue their activities. In January 1980, EPSA 2 led to an increase in the number of the subsidiaries of international companies. The diplomatic tension between Libya and the United States, under the Reagan administration, led to a withdrawal of American companies which in due course became complete. To make up for the absence of the Americans, Libya encouraged more local subsidiaries. In 1988, the new framework, EPSA 3, was devised to stimulate more investment. The Italian company SELM/Shell was one of the earliest to be granted an exploration license under the new arrangements. Further foreign companies made deals: these included Lasmo (London and Scottish Marine Oil), Hardy Oil and Gas, Red Sea Oil, the Yugoslav company INA Naftaplin, Braspetro/OMV/ Husky Oil and Gas (owned by Brazilian, Austrian and Canadian interests) and the Petrofina Group (consisting of Lasmo, Pedco and Agip).[43] The regime had achieved its foreign policy objective. Libya had established significant and influential linkages sufficient to hold at bay the policy of sanctions favoured by the United States.[44] Thus, despite the UN sanctions, Libya was an ongoing field of activity for the international oil companies, which continued to make substantial new oil finds.

The departure of the American companies in the 1980s, therefore, contributed substantially to the profits of the European companies which had maintained their presence in Libya in defiance of the UN sanctions and the unilateral American embargo. For the Europeans, Libya had become — in the same way as Algeria — a country of key importance in European energy policy. Its reserves of oil and gas had always attracted the European oil companies, whose goal was to position themselves ready for the moment when the sanctions were definitively lifted. The good relations Libya enjoyed with Germany and Italy helped to avoid an escalation of the sanctions. Meanwhile, the European oil companies assisted Libya to maintain its oil production, despite the effects of the international sanctions. During the sanctions period, the European companies grasped the opportunity afforded by the tension between Libya and the United States, taking their chance to invest substantially in Libya. The presence of the European companies protected the Libyan regime from the United States, while keeping up the level of production and enabling Libya to develop its ties with the political leadership of European states. However critical Libya might be of European governments, therefore, the oil companies continued to find a welcome in the country.

144   IS THE JAMAHIRIYA REFORMABLE?

Production of foreign companies in bpd (NOC, 202)

Operating groups	2001	2000	1999	1998	1997	1996	1995	1994	1993	NOC %
Agip	65.4	64.6	62.7	70.3	78.5	83.5	80.2	84.5	95.5	62.5
Arabian Gulf	136.8	144.3	149.6	163.7	151.1	177.3	156.7	154	150.7	100
Sirte	42.1	40.5	41.2	42.7	43.8	44.3	43.4	2	44.3	100
Veba	32.6	32.7	32.6	34.6	35.0	38.5	36.3	45.8	44.3	51.0
Waha	107.2	108.2	113.6	132.0	138.7	143.4	145.0	33.5	143.8	51.0
Zuweitina	26.0	25.4	24.5	25.5	25.6	27.0	27.1	146	26.8	66.0
Wintershall	39.9	39.4	39.4	42.3	32.9	31.2	20.4	5	13.0	51.0
Total	6.5	6.4	6.4	5.1	3.7	3.5	1.5	28.5		80.0
OMV	0.6	0.6	0.6	1.0		1.5		15.8		65
Repsol	59.7	58.1	56.5	32.6						50
Vina			0.4	0.9						
	516.800	519.800	527.700	550.900	509.200	549.9	510.600	508.800	518.400	

An examination of Libya's oil policy reveals that the regime was easily able to build up the relationships that were necessary to sustain it. Libya's energy policy satisfied the regime's foreign policy requirements: namely, the consolidation of ties with Europe, the return of the American oil companies, and the enhancement of Libya's image. On the other hand, the regime's energy production failed to meet its industrial needs. Libya has a network of international links that have enabled it to carry through its "conversion". However, the regime does not possess sufficient oil infrastructure to fulfil its wish to achieve the level of production before the nationalisation of oil and gas in 1970. Nevertheless, Libya's oil industry is still highly attractive.[45]

The economic costs of Libya's revolutionary policy

The regime's revolutionary policy has stood in the way of Libya's economic development. In the mid-1970s Libya had been "on the verge of occupying fourth place in world oil production, even though it entirely lacked an industrial base."[46] Thirty years later, history shows that the revolutionary regime has invested more in the development of its foreign policy than in the establishment of a modern oil industry. In 1969, Libya's revolutionary regime inherited the oil industry from the monarchy of King Idris, but — in contrast to the Gulf monarchies[47] and Algeria[48] — Libya failed to develop its inheritance.[49] For thirty years, Libya's productive capacity has been in decline. From 3.3

million barrels per day (bpd) in 1970, production fell by 57 per cent
to 1.4 million bpd by 1992, and has remained stable at that level. The
decline by comparison with the 1970s results from the production
quotas assigned by OPEC, to which Libya has broadly adhered. The
effects of the sanctions particularly affected the equipment owned by
the NOC, whose oil fields were the oldest and which were especially
hard hit by the lack of spare parts. The NOC's production capacity dropped by 30 per cent between 1992 and 1997, falling from
1.27 million bpd to 0.9 million bpd. This fall was made up for by
the increasing activity of the foreign operators, and in particular the
Europeans. In order to maintain the interest of the foreign companies,
the NOC has so far absorbed for the most part — up to 70 per cent
— the reduction in the OPEC quotas. A final consideration is that
most of Libya's known reserves were discovered between 1957 and
1967, accounting for 79 billion barrels out of its 113 billion barrels
of known reserves. The Sirte Basin, which has been most explored,
contains 87 per cent of the known reserves, as against only three per
cent in the Murzuq Basin, one of the most promising new areas for
exploration.[50]

Colonel Gaddafi's coup in 1969 had major consequences for the oil
and gas industry.[51] In 1972-73, the Libyan government nationalised
the hydrocarbon sector and terminated the hegemony of the foreign
companies — some 42 in all — which had dominated oil production
since the discovery of oil in 1959.[52] In 1979, the NOC was reorganised
to facilitate easier change in the oil sector. In 1986, the NOC achieved
a degree of autonomy from the General People's Committee, thanks
to the reassignment to it of the powers of the Petroleum Secretariat.
The nationalisation of oil and gas gave a substantial boost to the income
of the government. This was why, from the 1970s onward, Libya was
able to invest in five sectors regarded as being of key importance.
These were the oil and petrochemical industry; agriculture and water; iron and steel production; infrastructure; education and health.[53]
Immediately after the coup of 1969, Libya was a country with no

industry. There was only one refinery and a limited agricultural and food sector. The Libyan development plan of 1972-1975 was the first three-year plan to emphasise the importance of industry.[54] The Libyan authorities envisaged the development of heavy industry, based on petrochemical products. Two major projects which still stand as examples of this policy are the petrochemical complex of Ras Lanuf (which refines 11 million tonnes of the 18 million tonnes of crude oil refined annually in Libya); and the Misurata steelworks. However, the industrial sector as a whole represents only ten per cent of GDP. The fall in oil revenue in the 1980s and the United Nations sanctions in the 1990s substantially reduced the ability of the Libyan authorities to bring to fruition their investment plans in strategic sectors of the economy. The NOC says its production capacity is 1.7 million bpd, as against the 1.323 million bpd to which OPEC limits it. In fact, the NOC operates in a climate of the decline of its ability to produce.[55]

The embryonic oil industry launched in the 1970s was not sufficient for the construction of an industrial base able to provide the materials and the technology necessary for the further development of the oil sector. In the realm of oil infrastructure — exploration, drilling and pipelines — most construction dates from the period of the monarchy. From 1961 to 1970, Esso, Oasis, Mobil, BP and Occidental built pipelines, linking the main oilfields — including Zelten, Raguba, and Waha — to the terminals at Mersa Brega, Es-Sidr, Ras Lanuf, Harega, and Zuweitina. The western oilfields were linked to the terminals by pipelines constructed in the period 1976-1980 by the NOC. In general, foreign contractors had been responsible for the construction of even the non-oil economic infrastructure. The circumstances in which the Great Underground River project was planned and launched, with an initial budget of 30 billion dollars, serve as a comment on Libya's industrial self-sufficiency. The work had to be carried out — with some difficulty — by the South Korean company Dong Ah Construction. The high level of Libya's dependence on foreign contractors is surprising, given its former foreign policy of confrontation with the West. It might even be supposed that Libya's critical stance towards the West could have its origin in its inability to free itself of dependence on foreign companies, in spite of the nationalist policy of the 1970s.

The end of the Algerian model of development

While Gaddafi's nationalism shows the influence of Egypt's President Nasser,[56] the pattern on which the oil industry was built came from Algeria.[57] Gérard Destanne de Bernis explains Libya's choice: "Libya had at the outset no experience or industrial background. It would have been obliged completely to reinvent its population to cope with the most sophisticated technology and science." Cooperation between Libya and Algeria in the hydrocarbon sector began when Gaddafi took power. In the 1970s, the two countries planned to adopt a common position in dealing with the foreign companies in order to safeguard their interests, while coordinating their efforts to develop their national economies. Cooperation was established between Sonatrach and LIPETCO (which became LINOCO in 1970 and was finally transformed into the NOC). The two countries envisaged the exchange of information, technicians and experts, together with the creation of joint companies for research, and the production and transportation of oil. In practice, the management of the NOC was to copy Sonatrach's model, turning the NOC into an instrument by means of which the State regained power over the country's natural resources. The NOC followed Sonatrach's lead in three specific ways, to free itself from the foreign companies. These were the enhancement of investment; the development of engineering skills, reducing dependence and stipulating maximum use of local products; and the development of services. In 1971, Sonatrach's nationalisation of Algeria's oil fields and means of transportation, together with the increase in its holdings in joint ventures to 15 per cent, brought the result that Sonatrach controlled 75 per cent of Algeria's oil production and all its production of gas. Libya's objective was to enjoy economic development based on a control of resources on the model of the Algeria of Boumedienne, who was in power from 1965 to 1979.

In the 1980s, Sonatrach and the NOC signed accords on cooperation. On 11 November 1988, Algeria and Libya signed an agreement enabling the establishment of two joint ventures. These were the Arab Libyan-Algerian Exploration and Production Company (ALEPCO), whose remit was oil exploration, and the Libyan-Algerian Geophysics Company. The outcome of this cooperative enterprise was the discovery of an oil well at Oued Merabia in north-western Algeria, in the Hassi Messaoud oilfield. In November 1999, Sonatrach and the NOC planned a further joint venture involving the exploration of blocks of territory close to the common border of both countries.[58] Libya was also keen to develop its transport network, signing cooperation agreements with Algeria, Tunisia and Egypt. Further joint companies were created, including the Arab Maghreb Company for Gas and Transportation and Production, and the Arab Company for Engineering Consultancy. However, none of these agreements resulted in a profitable partnership for the two countries. Both Algeria and Libya faced economic problems and, unexpectedly found themselves once more in competition to supply Europe's wants.

The two countries had substantial reserves of gas, whose principal market was Europe. Libya was substantially behind in the exploitation of its gas. Algeria initiated the exploitation, production and commercialisation of its gas resources in the 1970s, while Libyan exploitation did not really get under way until 1990. Libya suffered from a marked lack of gas production infrastructure by comparison with the plant at Algeria's disposal. The Italian company Agip, however, worked to unify the gas sector across North Africa. Its objective, working through Agip North African and Middle East Ltd, was to bring about a convergence between the energy policies of Algeria and Libya.[59]

Modelling its approach on French policy in Algeria, Italy aimed to become the "patron" of the new Libya. For this scheme, Italy had considerable advantages. Through the medium of Agip, it had already maintained for decades a privileged partnership with Libya. With European energy demands in mind, Italy attempted to coordinate both Algerian and Libyan gas producers.[60] Libya had an obvious interest in linking its gas fields in part to the Algerian transport network. The question remained whether it was in Algeria's interest to develop its operations on a joint basis. In the short term, Algeria might certainly have been concerned to see a rival gas producer emerging in North Africa, but over the longer term it could exploit its position by becoming the recognised passageway for gas to Europe by way of the Transmed pipeline, opened in 1983. The construction of 1385 kilometres of pipeline from Hassi R'Mel, running thence through Morocco and on to Cordoba in Spain, at a time when there was a hostile relationship between Algeria and Morocco, had shown how the convergence of interests had taken precedence. Libya and Algeria also had a clear interest in aligning their positions in the international gas market. On the basis of their experience of the oil industry, Sonatrach and the Libyan NOC coordinated their approach in order to consolidate and reinforce their positions. In this regard, it can be said that the achievement of these companies in oil production was repeated in terms of gas. As events turned out, the consolidation of the Euro Mediterranean zone progressively increased the pressure on the states south of the Mediterranean to pursue convergent policies. The example of the construction of the Transmed pipeline showed that the establishment of regional coordination had consequences for bilateral relations between countries — in this case Morocco and Algeria.

Libya became the new gas provider in the Euromed region. The ministerial declaration of the Euromed energy forum in May 2003 stressed the need to complete the "Euromed circle of gas production" during the period 2003-200 by reinforcing the support of the Euromed region's collective support for a number of projects.[61] These included a new gas pipeline from Algeria serving Spain and France; a gas pipeline from Algeria serving Italy and France; a gas pipeline from Libya serving

Italy and passing through Malta; as well as linkages in the gas networks between Egypt, Libya and Tunisia.

The Libyan regime was well aware of the advantages of its geographical position, but it was also conscious of European concerns over the threats to stability and security faced by the countries of the southern shore of the Mediterranean. The Libyan regime's energy policy was a powerful antidote: Libya's progressive absorption into the circle of oil and gas providers protected it against any criticism that might be raised regarding human rights violations or restrictions on political freedom. As did the regime's other basic organs, the oil sector introduced changes which were in line with the regime's overall programme. It reacted to the need to sustain a government damage by ten years of sanctions. In this context, Libya's oil income was an extremely important factor, which set the scene for the rehabilitation of a regime regarded until very recently as a "pariah state".[62]

Conclusion

A new administrative class has taken control of the machinery of the Libyan State. Its intention is to transform Libya into an ally of the western powers, specifically the Europeans and the Americans. This group believes that Libya has the resources required to become a Mediterranean power. They take their inspiration from the Gulf States, who have benefited from their excellent relations with the West whilst maintaining authoritarian political systems controlled by the members of a single family. As the new decision makers see it, Libya positioned itself on the wrong side in the 1970s, and the policy of the revolutionary regime went astray, wasting the regime's resources. 11 September 2001 was a historic opportunity for Libya to place itself on the "good" side: that of the United States. Meanwhile the entanglement of the US in Iraq provided an opportunity for Libya to cash in on its oil sector and its unexploited reserves. The liberalisation of the hydrocarbon sector was part of a public relations exercise intended to consolidate Libya's position in the "good" camp of the western powers.

However, the process of liberalisation of Libya's economy has so far had consequences in the sphere of politics. The "conversion" of the regime to the New World Order has had no immediate effect on Libya's political system. Control over the oil revenue is still tightly restricted to the immediate circles of decision makers who surround Colonel Gaddafi. Meanwhile the redistribution of a portion of the oil revenue enables the regime to lubricate the wheels of those parts of its machinery which continue to perform the function of coercion: the Revolutionary Committees and the Jamahiriya Guard. The opening up of the hydrocarbon sector to foreign participation will lead to a substantial increase in the income from oil. In the last resort, this will substantially reinforce the financial power of the Gaddafi family over the Libyan State and Libyan society. In this sense, liberalisation has become a mechanism by which the regime has consolidated itself rather than an economic process conducive to the reinforcement of democracy.

CONCLUSION
AFTER GADDAFI?

Towards what political models is the Libyan oil State drawn? The Libyan regime is in the process of making changes which reveal its powerful capacity to adapt. Under the sanctions, the regime closed ranks, excluding all but members of the clans closest to Muammar Gaddafi, in order better to combat the Islamist groups which threatened it. A gathering sentiment of vulnerability prompted the re-organisation of the security institutions and the replacement of those in charge of the security services. The regime survived, however, overcoming the three challenges it faced: armed Islamist dissidence, the international sanctions, and a series of coup attempts. It then went on to seize the twin opportunities presented by the events of 11 September and the American-led invasion of Iraq. An accomplished tactician, Gaddafi signed Libya up to the "global war against terror", creating an image of his country as a kind of Mediterranean Eldorado, which contrasted favourably with the hallucination of oil in Iraq. In parallel with this process of "conversion", Libya has adopted a new rhetoric, speaking in terms of transparency, of the struggle against corruption, and of democracy. It remains the case, however, that future investors will continue to need patience and understanding to work in Libya.[1]

Libya's transformation is taking place against the background of a political context in which the succession to power of Gaddafi's son Seif el-Islam has taken on great significance. In this light, the changes which are observable in Libya represent, in some sense, a process of reversion to the norm for regimes in the region. The changes do not amount to alterations in the Libyan system, nor are they a clean break with the past. They more resemble the adoption of a new kind of relationship. The regime possesses two resources which it expertly markets: its intimate knowledge of terrorism and its oil reserves. These resources give it the elbow-room to "convert" itself without real transformation. Unexpectedly, the lifting of the ban on arms sales to Libya has restored the country to the status of a profitable market for the arms industry. Constant visits to Tripoli by Europe's political leaders indicate how highly Libya is now rated. But has the regime staying power? Are the promised reforms credible? And, faced by changes within the regime, how will the centres of power be transformed?

The Libyan regime embarked on changes as the result of pressure from three directions: the international sanctions, Islamist unrest, and the threat of invasion. Under the sanctions, from 1992 to 2003, the regime experienced a sensation which was new to it: that of an extreme vulnerability, which impelled it to make alterations. Islamist violence, which lasted from 1995 and 1998, was a factor which undermined the Jamahiriya's confidence that it could survive in the new international circumstances. But what especially alarmed it was the overthrow of Saddam Hussein. Up to then, the international sanctions had not greatly concerned the regime, and Colonel Gaddafi had seemed attracted by the idea of turning Libya into a kind of Mediterranean Cuba. In 2003, a gust of panic was felt in Tripoli, which blew away the regime's certainty that it could withstand simultaneously the pressure of Islamist violence from within at the same times as the threat of invasion from without. On the other hand, from the revolution of 1969 up to the present day, the security apparatus had shown its ability to protect the regime from internal threats. The Jamahiriya, however, was a police state rather than a military regime, and while its security forces were very capable in the field of political control and repression, they were seriously inadequate in the military sphere. The invasion of Iraq appeared to indicate the possibility of a direct confrontation with the United States. The Libyan regime would have been helpless in such an eventuality, as Iraq's regime had been. The link between the Libyan administration and a nexus of tribal clans was a powerful protection against internal threats. The government's authority was founded on the absolute loyalty of their members. But in the case of a conventional war, the government would no longer be able to rely on its citizens, and still less on its army, which it regarded with profound mistrust.

All these factors led to the "conversion" of the Libyan regime, which — chameleon-like — adapted itself to the nature of its surroundings. The possibility that the regime might fall signalled the end of the governmental role of the Gaddafa tribe. The clans affiliated to the Gaddafa committed themselves as a group to the transformation of the regime in key sectors including oil and gas, and security. Libya's "conversion" proceeded with alacrity, and it took care to emphasise the convergence of its interests in all spheres with those of the United States and Europe. It terminated its WMD programme, and exhorted other regimes to do likewise. It liberalised its oil sector, while offering Europe guaranteed energy supplies. The inauguration of the West Jamahiriya Gas Project on 7 October 2004 set the seal on the new relationship between Libya and Europe. As a Libyan statement put it: "We declare before the world that Italy and Libya have decided to create in the Mediterranean a sea of peace. The Mediterranean will be a sea of trade and tourism, a sea under which oil and gas pipelines will pass through Libya and Italy to link Africa and Europe."[2] Similarly, in response to Europe's unease on the issue of migration, Libya expressed its readiness to accept "secure centres" on its soil. In February 2003, Tony Blair proposed the idea of notion of creating protection zones outside Europe. In August 2004 Otto Schily, the German Minister of the Interior, and his Italian counterpart Giuseppe Pisanu, took up the idea, with a proposal to set up "closed centres", which would in effect be camps where migrants' requests for asylum would be scrutinised.[3]

On the threshold of the 21st century, the goal of Colonel Gaddafi's regime was to position itself on the "good" side — that of the United States and its allies. In the view of Seif el-Islam, Gaddafi's probable successor, Libya — rather than repeating the errors of the past — should exploit its advantages, offering its new allies the energy supplies they require, together with cooperation in the fields of security and migration. The new leaders who had made their appearance in the oil and security sectors, mainly educated in the United States, gradually pushed aside the old "revolutionaries", with their eastern European training, who had taken the view that Libya's vocation lay in Africa or the Arab world. In the view of these new leaders, Libya should attach itself firmly to the West. The question was how to dismantle the revolutionary regime without disturbance. The old regime still had its "guard dogs", resistant to change.

However, on 3 March 2006, when Al-Baghdadi Ali Mahmoudi was appointed Prime Minister in succession to Shukri Ghanem, a question mark seemed to come into view over the future of Shukri Ghanem's agenda of liberalisation. The "revolutionaries" had begun to fear that political reforms would soon follow the planned economic reform. The events which took place in Benghazi on 17 February 2006 provide an indication of their concern. Demonstrators led by the Revolutionary Committees chanted anti-Italian slogans in front of the Italian consulate as a protest against the report that an Italian minister, Roberto Calderoli, had worn a T-shirt reproducing one of the notorious Danish anti-Islamic cartoons. Soon, anti-Gaddafi slogans were also heard, and the overwhelmed police force fired on the crowd, leaving eleven dead and 60 wounded. Following this incident, the regime's leading figures all went to Benghazi to calm the situation. The Minister of the Interior was dismissed for the "excessive use of force" and a number of Muslim Brothers from the Benghazi region, imprisoned since 1998, were freed. In early March, Gaddafi delivered one of his revolutionary addresses, reassuring the revolutionaries that no political reform was contemplated, and repeating his view that democracy and political parties were deviations to be condemned. Finally, he launched into a diatribe against the Italian colonial period (from 1911 to 1942) and demanded financial compensation for its consequences. The revolutionaries were evidently not yet ready to be sacrificial victims on the altar of reform.

Nevertheless, it continues to appear highly probable that the revolutionary regime's political and security structures may be progressive dismantled. The timetable appears to depend on how long Gaddafi remains in power. While Gaddafi lives, it seems probable that any dismantling will be very small in scale. However, the process has already begun with the liberation of certain political prisoners, followed by the abolition of the so-called "People's Court". In January 2005, a directive addressed by Colonel Gaddafi to the General People's Congress required the abolition of the People's Court, whose duty had been to conduct secret trials of those accused of political offences. In the opinion of the Libyan League for Human Rights: "The abolition of the 'People's Court' and the exceptional laws is undoubtedly a commendable step in the right direction, but should be followed by other measures if the purpose of their abolition is to remedy the deplorable human rights situation in Libya. In fact, respect for human rights has been obstructed not only by the 'People's Court' but, more particularly, by the total lack of an equitable and independent judiciary."[4]

On the other hand, after Gaddafi's demise, Seif el-Islam's Libya seems likely to follow the predictable route of an authoritarian liberal regime. In this respect, the constitution of the monarchical period may even be revived in order to bring back press freedom and the right of free association. The lifting of the international sanctions has led to the re-appearance of political demands. In March 2004, shortly before the visit to Tripoli by William Burns, the United State Assistant Secretary of State for Near Eastern Affairs, a document signed by 108 representatives of the Libyan opposition called for a catalogue of reforms in Libya: "The creation of constitutional rule chosen by the people of their own free will, and the dissolution of all legislation, structures and organizations that deviate from or contradict this constitutional legal framework; the establishment of democratic principles, the rule of law and the independence of the judiciary; the guaranteeing of political participation in the decision-making process, the democratic selection of leaders, and the implementation and respect of the principle that governments change; the release of all political prisoners of conscience, and the shedding of light on the fate all citizens who have been kidnapped or have disappeared; the abrogation of all laws that were established to cause oppression and curb freedoms etc."[5]

Libya's future may lie in a synthesis between the monarchy, as it existed under King Idris from 1951 to 1969, and the revolutionary regime. Post-Gaddafi Libya would therefore combine the attractions of a consumer society open to the world with the constraints of an authoritarian liberal regime anxious to maintain its power.

NOTES

PREFACE

[1] US Department of State, "US Diplomatic Relations with Libya" http://www.state.gov/secretary/rm/2006/66235.htm

[2] Cited by Yahyia H. Zoubir in "The United States and Libya: From Confrontation to Normalization," *Middle East Policy* XIII: 2, Summer 2006, p. 57

[3] Martin Indyk, "The Iraq War did not force Gadaffi's Hand," http://www.brookings.edu/views/op-ed/indyk/20040309.htm

INTRODUCTION

[†] Gaddafi's "State of the Masses" — the word derives from the Arabic word "jamahir", which means "the masses".

[1] Michel Camau and Vincent Geisser, *Le syndrome autoritaire*, Paris: Presses de Sciences-Po, 2003.

[2] Yasuyuki Matsunaga, "L'Etat rentier est-il réfractaire à la démocratie?" *Critique Internationale*, no.8, July 2000.

[3] Eva Bellin, "The Robustness of Authoritarianism in the Middle East: Exceptionalism in Comparative Perspective", *Comparative Politics*, vol. 26, no. 2, January 2004; Michel Camau and Vincent Geisser, *op.cit.* Philippe Droz-Vincent, "Quel avenir pour l'autoritarisme dans le monde arabe?", *Revue Française de Sciences Politiques*, December 2004.

[4] Daniel Brumberg, "Democratization in the Arab World: The Trap of Liberalized Democracy," *Journal of Democracy*, vol. 13, no. 4, October 2000; Larbi Sadiki, *The Search for Arab Democracy*, London: Hurst, 2004; Steve Heydemann, "La question de la démocratie dans les travaux sur le monde arabe",*Critique Internationale*, October 2002.

[5] Hazem Beblawi, "The Rentier State in the Arab World", in Hazem Beblawi and Giacomo Luciani (eds) *The Rentier State*, London: Croom Helm, 1987.

6 See the critical analysis offered by Michael L. Ross, "The Political Economy of the Resource Curse", *World Politics*, 15, January 1999.

7 Theda Skocpol points out the massive scale of military spending by rentier States. Theda Skocpol, "Rentier States and Shi'a Islam in the Iranian Revolution", *Theory and Society*, no. 11, April 1982.

8 Clement M. Henry, "Algeria's Agonies: Oil Rent Effects in a Bunker State", *the Journal of North African Studies*, vol. 9, no. 2, Summer, 2004.

9 Karl Terry Lynn, *The Paradox of Plenty: Oil Booms and Petro-States*, Berkeley: University of California Press, 1997; Michael L. Ross, "Does Oil Hinder Democracy", *World Politics*, 53, April 2001.

10 Rémy Leveau, "*Le système politique, La Libye nouvelle. Rupture et continuité*, Paris: CNRS, 1975, p.85.

11 Quoted by Leonard S.Spector, *Nuclear Ambitions: the Spread of Nuclear Weapons*, Boulder: Westview Press, 1990, p.183.

12 "The concept [of a rogue state] had its origin in the idea of a 'pariah' or 'outcast' in international relations. The British imported this term from India in the colonial period. During the 1960s and 1970s, a number of authors used similar terminology to describe particular States whose behaviour did not conform to international norms. However, it was in the 1980s that the concept of 'rogue State' as it is used today came into use. Hitherto the expressions, 'terrorist States' or 'outlaw States' had been used. In 1986 US President Ronald Reagan was already advocating the total isolation of terrorist States. This was a policy aimed primarily at Colonel Gaddafi's 'outlaw' regime in Libya." Jean-François Rancourt, "Rogue State: un concept incompatible avec la politique étrangère", *Points de Mire*, vol. 6, no. 1, 19 January 2005.

13 The sanctions "consisted of an embargo on all flights originating in Libya, unless authorised, as well as an embargo on arms, weapons and any military materiel or assistance. In addition, the Security Council called on all Member States of the United Nations to limit the number of Libyan diplomatic and consular staff in their territory and not to offer asylum to any Libyan terrorist. Finally, it called for the closure of all offices of Libya Arab airlines.... [On 11 November 1993, the Council declared in Resolution 883:] "after 20 months the Libyan government had still not complied with its demands.... The Council demanded the freezing of all funds and other financial resources outside Libya held or controlled directly or indirectly by the Libyan government or by Libyan public authorities of Libya, or any Libyan undertaking. This embargo did not, however, relate to any funds derived from the sale of petroleum or the supply of petroleum, gas products, commodities or agricultural products." Sandrine Santo, "L'ONU face au terrorisme", Groupe de recherche et d'information sur la paix et la sécurité, Rapport 2001/5.2, www.grip.org/pub/rapports/rg01-5_onu.pdf, p.16.

14 Libya benefited from Saudi mediation in the resolution of this dispute, a consideration to which the then Crown Prince of Saudi Arabia Abdullah Ibn Abdelaziz did not fail to refer in his verbal altercation with the Libya leader Colonel Gaddafi at the Arab League summit on 1 March 2003.

[15] Moncef Djaziri sums up: "After the explosion of the Pan Am Boeing above Lockerbie in Scotland on 21 December 1988, with 270 deaths, a criminal trial took place under American auspices in cooperation with Scottish judges. This lasted three years and involved visits to 70 countries, 15,000 witness statements and more than 20 million dollars in expenses. It reached conclusions which implicated two Libyan citizens, Abdel Basset Ali al-Megrahi and Amin Khlifa Fhima." *Annuaire de l'Afrique du Nord*, CNRS Editions, 1998.

[16] The six were Abdallah Elzragh, first counsellor at the Libyan Embassy in Brazzaville, Ibrahim Naeli and Arbas Musbah, members of the Libyan secret service, Abdelsalam Issa Shibani, a technical official in the intelligence service, Abdelsalam Hammouda, and Abdallah Senoussi, Gaddafi's brother-in-law, who was number two in the secret service.

1. THE END OF THE EMBARGO

[1] "The Impact of the UN Sanctions Against Libya", September 1996 www.libya-watanona.com/libya1/

[2] "Les effects de l'embargo sur les finances extérieures de la Libye". *Marchés tropicaux*, 11 September, 1998, p.1907

[3] "Any product which produces inebriation shall be described as 'Hamra' whatever may be the quantity consumed or the alcoholic content of the product. It is forbidden to consume any such product, or to procure it, sell it, make it, offer it, or give it." See: *Annuaire de l'Afrique du Nord,* Legislative section 1994-95, vol. 34, 1995. p. 619.

[4] Meliha B. Altunisik, "A rentier state's response to oil crisis: economic reform policies in Libya", *Arab Studies Quarterly*, vol. 18, no.4, 1996.

[5] "The sale of hydrocarbons represented 25 per cent of GDP, 50 per cent of budgetary receipts and 95 per cent of current account receipts." *Marchés tropicaux et méditerranéens*, 6 September 1996.

[6] Dirk Vandewalle, "Qadhafi's Perestroika: Economic and Political Liberalization in Libya", *The Middle East Journal*, 45, 1991, no.2; François Burgat, "1989: l'ouverture entravée", *Annuaire de l'Afrique du Nord*, vol. 27, Paris: CNRS, 1991.

[7] Ariel Colonnomos, *La morale dans les relations internationales*, Paris: Odile Jacob, 2005, p. 128.

[8] "Les effects de l'embargo sur les finances extérieures de la Libye", *Marchés tropicaux*, 11 September 1998.

[9] From *Marchés tropicaux*, 11 September 1998.

[10] In 1999, the government estimated the rate of unemployment at 11 per cent. In reality, it was between 20 and 30 per cent. A parallel economy sprang up in response to the economic crisis. In 1996, the Jamahiriya took steps against the development of unofficial trading, with "Purification Committees" in charge of "stamping out the scourge" of speculation. A law provided for the death penalty for "any persons performing currency exchange operations in violation of the regulations of the Central

162 NOTES [pp. 17-26]

Bank" and for those practising "speculation in foodstuffs, clothing, housing and transport." Eric Gobe, "Libya", *Annuaire de l'Afrique du Nord*, Volume 35, 1996, CNRS, p. 510

11 Dirk Vandewalle, *Libya since Independence: Oil and State-Building*, Cornell University Press, 1998.

12 The quotations from Colonel Gaddafi given here were unofficially communicated to the author.

13 A model in which the net receipts of the oil sector are place in an "Oil Fund" which invests them in a diverse portfolio of international holdings.

14 In 1998 the majority of the ministries were transferred from Tripoli to the towns of Benghazi, Kufra and Sirte.

15 The members of the government appointed on 1 March 2000 were: Mubarak al-Shameikh (Secretary-General of the General Popular Committee), Bashir Bou-Janah (Deputy Prime Minister for Production), Baghdadi Mahmudi (Deputy Prime Minister for Services), Abd al-Rahman Shalqam (Minister of Foreign Affairs and Cooperation), Mrs Fawzia Bashir Shalabi (Minister of Information, Culture and Tourism), Ali al-Triki (Minister for African Unity), Mohammed al-Zawi (Minister of Justice and Security), and Jad al-Tahli (Minister for Planning).

16 The remaining ministers were: Foreign Affairs – Suleyman Sassi al-Shuhumi; Economy and Trade – Shukri Mohammed Ghanem; Finance – Ajuli Brini; Justice and Security – Mohammed Musrati; African Unity – Abdessalaam Triki.

17 *Welfare in the Mediterranean Countries,* Great Popular Socialist Libyan Jamahiriya. www.unpan.org.

18 Bashir S. Ghariany, "State of Public Administration in Libya", Paper delivered at Consultative Meeting on Priorities in Innovating Governance and Administration in the Euro-Mediterranean Region, 17-20 May 2004, UN Department of Economic and Social Affairs, Centre for Administrative Innovation in the Mediterranean Region (CAIMED). http://unpanl.un.org/intradoc/groups/public/documents/un/unpan016111.cf.pdf

19 Ibid. According to decree 242 of August 1999, and Circular No.2, the Sha'biyat also enjoy the power to grant import and export licenses.

20 Omar I. El Fathaly and Monte Palmer, *Political Development and Social Change in Libya*, Toronto: Lexington Books, 1980, p. 28.

21 "L'urbanisation en Méditerranée de 1950 à 1995", *Les cahiers du plan*, 1, 2001, p. 3.

22 Libya: Higher Education Profile. www.bc.edu/bc.

23 Hervé Bleuchot, *Chroniques et documents libyens (1969-1980)*, Paris: CNRS, 1983, p. 90.

24 Radio France Internationale, report, 11 October 2000.

25 Agence France Presse, 1 November 2000.

26 In his Third Universal Theory Gaddafi rejects democracy and the multiparty system in favour of political and economic egalitarianism. Political parties are banned because "a party enables a minority to seize the power which belongs to the people. Joining a party is a betrayal of the people: a party supporter is guilty of treachery. The people

now express themselves through the Basic People's Congresses. In economic terms, employees become associates: "They are associated with the ownership of productive institutions. See Hervé Bleuchot, "Le Livre Vert: son contexte, sa signification. *Maghreb-Machrek*, no. 93, July-August, 1981, p. 23

27 The construction of Gaddafi as a charismatic figure dates back to the earliest days: "Once the dust of the Revolution had settled, Qadhafi moved quickly to create an image of strength and dynamism. Libya's sizeable Italian community was given very short notice to leave the country. Their sizeable property holdings, including much of the finest agricultural land in Libya, were confiscated. Italian churches were closed or turned into mosques. The grand Cathedral in Tripoli was converted into a mosque and presented to non-Arab Muslims as their international headquarters. Qadhafi claimed final victory over the Italians, the primary symbol of Libyan inferiority or humiliation. In much the same manner, leases for British and American Bases, also symbols of foreign domination, were ordered terminated.... In subsequent years, Qadhafi has reinforced his image as as an international giant killer repeatedly baiting the major powers of the West." Omar I. El Fathaly and Monte Palmer, *Political Development and Social Change in Libya*, op. cit., 1980, p. 64.

28 Arabs from other countries are not regarded as foreigners in Libya and may live there without visas.

29 Relations with Tunisia had been strained and suspicious from the stillborn Tunisian-Libyan union in the so-called "Arab Islamic Republic" in 1974 up to the Gafsa incidents of 1980 and the massive expulsion of Tunisian workers in 1985. Libya's relations with Egypt had been hostile from the 1973 war up to the expulsion of 300,000 Egyptian workers. See: Elysabeth Stemer, "La fusion Tuniso-libyenne", *Maghreb-Machrek*, 1974, no. 62; and Pierre Rondot, "Libye et Maghreb Arabe", *Défense nationale*, vol. 45, November 1989; Nicole Grimaud, "Tunisiens en Libye: quand les migrants sont pris en otage", *Hommes et migration*, no. 1174, March 1992.

30 Gaddafi explained his association agreement with Egypt and Sudan in 1970 as follows: "Libya has money, Sudan has land and Egypt has men." According to some estimates, the number of foreigners in Libya is in the neighbourhood of one and a half million (of whom a million are Egyptian, 300,000 Sudanese and 200,000 foreigners of various origins, including the Maghreb states, Syria and Pakistan).

31 The "Islamic Legion" consists of some 2500 men, and was set up for the purpose of foreign interventions, especially in Chad. Its fighters are of Arab and African origin and are recruited among the migrant workers, who if they refuse the offer may be threatened with the death penalty: in 1988 20 African residents were hanged for refusing to enlist. See: J-F Daguzan, *Le dernier rempart? Forces armées et politiques de défense au Maghreb*, Paris: Publisud, 1998.

32 René Otayek, *La politique africaine de la Libye*, Paris: Karthala, 1987.

33 The Revolutionary Committees were established in November 1977. They were "the guardians of the Revolution. The members of the People's Congresses, as well as other leaders, were no less patriotic or indeed revolutionary than the Revolutionary Committees, but the latter declared that they were henceforth ready to die for

the defence and consolidation of the Revolution." (Quoted from a speech by Colonel Gaddafi made in February 1978). The Revolutionary Committees laid down guidelines for the Basic Popular Committees, encouraged the Basic Popular Congresses to consolidate the authority of the people, exhorting the people to exercise their power and keeping the objectives of the Revolution before the public eye. See Habib el-Hasnawi, "The Revolutionary Committees and their Role in the Confirmation and Consolidation of the People's Authority", *Political, Economic and Social Bases of the Third Universal Theory*, Seminar, Belgrade, April 1982. Proceedings published by the World Centre for Research and Study on the Green Book, Tripoli.

34 According to Moncef Ouannes, "The young men underwent a probationary period which was often difficult, including making reports on neighbours, classmates and family members, and involvement in the torture of opposition figures and the pursuit of Islamists. See "Les Comités Revolutionnaires: mouvement social ou expression clientéliste?" *Revue tunisienne de sciences sociales*, No. 116, 1994.

35 In a statement made to the press in September 1998, Gaddafi said: "I have tried everything, and made many sacrifices but the Arabs are immobilised by defeatism and humiliation, failing to seek their liberty or their dignity, and seeming unable to stand up to the United States and Israel." *L'Autre Afrique*, 18-25 March 1998.

36 Following the decision by France, Spain and Italy to establish a multinational force at division strength, to be known as Eurofor, as well as a pre-structured and non-permanent multinational naval force (Euromarfor), Abdelwahab Biad has noted that "Libya has condemned a military operation targeting the Arab nation." See "Les pays du Sud de la Méditerrannée et l'avènement d'une politique de défense européenne", *Connections Quarterly Journal*, no. 1, 2001, p. 53.

37 In June 1998, in Tunis, US Under-Secretary of State Stuart Eizenstat proposed a partnership between the United States and the three countries of the Maghreb.

38 With the exception of the D'Amato Act, that provided for sanctions against enterprises investing more than 40 million dollars in either Libya or Iran.

39 In 1974, in the Green Book, Gaddafi explained that business should cease, since it was a form of exploitation. In practice, private business was a handicap for the Jamahiriya since it tended to promote the financial independence of individuals.

40 See: John O. Igue and Bio G. Soule, *L'Etat entrepôt au Benin*, Paris: Karthala, 1992.

41 Hassan Boubakri. "Echanges transfrontaliers et commerce parallèle aux frontières tuniso-libyennes", *Maghreb-Machrek*, no. 170, October 2000; p. 39.

42 Ibid.; and Hassen Boubakri and Mustapha Chandoul, "Migrations clandestines et contrebandes à la frontière tuniso-libyenne", *Revue européenne des migrations internationales*, No. 2, 1991.

43 In a speech in which Gaddafi condemned this "plundering" of the State, he declared that "it is not acceptable for a kilo of imported cheese which costs one dinar at the official price to be sold for eighteen times as much in shops in the private sector." *Marchés tropicaux et méditerranéens*, 6 September, 1996.

44 Béatrice Hibou, Jean-François Bayart, Stephen Ellis, *La criminalisation de l'Etat en Afrique*, Bruxelles: Complexe, 1997, p. 167.

45 Emmanuel Grégoire, "Réseaux et espaces économiques trans-étatiques", Réunion du Groupe d'Orientations des Politiques, July 2003, p. 11 www.oecd.org/dataoecd/23/62/25338394.pdf.

46 Emmanuel Grégoire, ibid. p. 12.

47 The author researched the situation on the boat between Tripoli and Malts three times between 1996 and 1998.

48 "Sida: la libération des bulgares est 'un test pour la Libye'", www.survivreausida.net, 17 January 2004.

49 "Le sida en progression en 2003 en Libye", www.survivreausida.net, 5 December 2003.

2. 11 SEPTEMBER 2001: THE "CONVERSION" OF THE REGIME

1 The US State Department report on international terrorism included six countries on the list: Cuba Iran, Iraq, Libya, North Korea and Sudan. These countries were under United States sanctions covering the export and sale of armaments, an economic and trade embargo, and the lifting of diplomatic immunity to permit action to be taken in the American courts by the families of victims of terrorist acts. "Patterns of Global Terrorism 2001", US State Department, www.state.gov.

2 "Musa Kusa, the head of Libya's spy agency, got the attention of Britain's foreign office and MI6 intelligence service when the he contacted them in March 2003 .... Kusa said Libya would agree to rid itself of all nuclear and chemical weapons and materials, along with longer-range missile delivery systems. Gaddafi's condition: Britain and the United States must help remove the sanctions on his regime and normalize relations with Libya." The Washington Times, "Libyan sincerity on arms in doubt", 9 September 2004.

3 Le Figaro, 28 April 2003.

4 According to Noam Chomsky, a secret report dating from 1995 shows that the United States changed its strategy of deterrence after the cold war by replacing the Soviet Union with the so-called rogue states: Iraq, Iran, Libya, Syria, Sudan, Cuba and North Korea. See: Noam Chomsky, "L'Amérique, 'Etat voyou'", Le Monde Diplomatique, August 2000.

5 For a French view of the Bush administration, see Bruno Tertrais, Quatre ans pour changer le monde: l'Amérique de G. Bush, 2005, 2008, Paris: Autrement, 2004.

6 For relations between Libya and Israel, see Jacob Abadi, "Pragmatism and rhetoric in Libya's policy towards Israel", The Journal of Conflict Studies, vol.200, No. 1, Fall 2000

7 ALFA letter to President Bush, www.defenddemocracy.org/research_topics/research_topics...

8 For example, Claudia Rosett, "Deal with the Devil", Wall Street Journal, 31 December 2003

9 www.whitehouse.gov/news/releases/2003/12, 19 December, 2003.

10 Said Haddad, "Les théatres non-africains de la géopolitique libyenne", *Annuaire de Afrique du Nord*, 38, 1999.

11 See Ronal E. Neumann: "Testimony before Senate Foreign Relations Sub-Committee for Near Eastern and South Asian Affairs", Deputy Assistant Secretary of State for Near Eastern Affairs Neumann, www.useu.be/ISSUES/neum.

12 The heads of Marathon, Amerada Hess, Conoco and Oxy held a number of meetings with Ahmed Abdulkarim, the Libyan official in charge of energy, with a view to arranging their return to Libya. *Maghreb Confidential*, 4 April 2002.

13 Yahya H. Zoubir, "Libya in US Foreign Policy", *Third World Quarterly*, vol. 23, no. 1, 2002.

14 Yahya Zoubir, "Libya in US foreign policy: from rogue state to good fellow", *Third World Quarterly*, vol. 23, no. 1, 2002.

15 Quoted by Yahya Zoubir, op. cit.

16 *News Telegraph*, 7 October 2001.

17 The LIFG was placed on the list of 37 "foreign terrorist organisations" by the Secretary of State. This meant that any assets it held in American financial institutions were frozen and any material support or provision of resources afforded to it by any citizen of the United States or any other person on United States territory would henceforth be regarded as a criminal offence. State Department, Office of Counterterrorism www.state.gov/s/ct/rls/fs/37191.htm.

18 "Testimony before the Senate Foreign Relations Sub-Committee for Near Eastern and South Asian Affairs". Ronald E. Neumann. www/useu.be/ISSUES/neum0504.

19 President George W. Bush said on 2 January 2003: "On January 7, 1986, President Reagan declared a national emergency to deal with the unusual and extraordinary threat to the national security and foreign policy of the United States constituted by the actions and policies of the Government of Libya. On January 8, 1986, the President took additional measures to block Libyan assets in the United States. The President has transmitted a notice continuing this emergency to the Congress and the Federal Register every year since 1986. The crisis between the United States and Libya that led to the declaration of a national emergency on January 7, 1986, has not been resolved.... Therefore, I am continuing for 1 year the national emergency with respect to Libya. This notice shall be published in the Federal Register and transmitted to the Congress." www.whitehouse/gov/news/releases/2003/1.

20 www.mees.com/postedarticles/politics/ArabPressReview.

21 Helmy Ibrahim, "La Libye ou l'institution politique du terrorisme", *Esprit*, no. 94-95; Allan Dowes, "Qu'est-ce qu'un Etat terroriste?", *Les cahiers de l'Orient*, no 36; St. John Ronald Bruce, "Terrorism and Libyan Foreign Policy, 1981-1986", *World Today*, no. 42, 1986.

22 In August 2000, the Mathaba ran a conference attended by Sam Nujoma (Namibia), Robert Mugabe (Zimbabwe), Yoweri Museveni (Uganda), Idris Deby (Chad), Shaffik Handal (FMLN, San Salvador), Daniel Ortega (FSLN, Nicaragua), Paul Reyes (FARC, Colombia), among others. Globalsecurity.org/intell/world/libya/jso.htm.

23 "Globalisation" became a dominant theme in Libya, gradually replacing the existing literature on anti-imperialism.
24 Stephen D. Collins, "Dissuading State Support of Terrorism: Strikes or Sanctions? An Analysis of Dissuasion Measures Employed Against Libya." *Studies in Conflict and Terrorism*, no. 27, 2004, p. 6
25 St.John Ronald Bruce, *Libya and the United States: two Centuries of Strife*, Philadelphia: University of Pennsylvania Press, 2002.
26 See the extremely detailed investigation carried out by Pierre Péan, who concludes that Iran was responsible. *Manipulations africaines. Qui sont les vrais coupables de l'attentat du vol UTA 772*, Paris: Plon, 2001.
27 "Between 1979 and 1983, Libyan imports of military hardware amounted to $12.095 million.... Between 1970 and 1985, total expenditures of overseas purchases of military goods and services at some $29 billion." William J. Foltz, "Libya's Military Power", in *The Green and the Black*, René Lemarchand (ed.), Indiana University Press, 1988, p. 62. See also, Anthony H. Cordesman, *A Tragedy of Arms:Military and Security Developments in the Maghreb*, Westport: Greenwood, 2001, p. 60.
28 *New York Times*, 18 February 2003. On 4 February 2003, Abdul Qadeer Khan the Pakistani "father of the bomb" confessed on television that he had provided Libya with the plans for constructing centrifuges. The *NYT* article uncovers the clandestine links which enabled Libya to obtain what it needed not only in Pakistan but also in Malaysia.
29 The German company Imhaisen-Chemie AG "played a central role in the building of the Rabta chemical complex", Joshua Sinai, "Libya's pursuit of WMD", *The Non-Proliferation Review*, Spring/Summer 1997, p. 94.
30 "Libya Has Trouble Building the Most Deadly Weapons", *The Risk Report*, vol. 1, December 1995.
31 William J. Foltz, "Libya's Military Power", op. cit., p. 53.
32 See René Lemarchand for a detailed analysis of Libya's policy of destabilisation of African regimes: René Lemarchand, "Beyond the Mad Dog Syndrome" in *The Green and the Black*, René Lemarchand (ed.) op. cit., p. 9.
33 globalsecurity.org/intell/world/libya/jso.htm.
34 Sandrine Santo, "L'ONU face au terrorisme", Groupe de recherche at d'information sur la paix et la sécurité, www.grip.org.
35 Philippe Moreau Defarges, "L'Etat voyou: un concept instrument", *Défense nationale*, no. 2, February 1998.
36 *Le Quotidien d'Oran*, 8 July 2003.
37 Among the "outposts of tyranny" were Iran, Cuba, Burma, North Korea, Belarus and Zimbabwe.
38 *El Hayat*, 14 June 1998.
39 Eric Gobe, "Libye: chronique intérieure", *Annuaire de l'Afrique du Nord*, vol.35, 1996, p. 503.
40 Ray Takeyh, "Qadhafi and the challenge of militant Islam", *The Washington Quarterly*, Summer 1998, p. 159.

168   NOTES   [pp. 57-66]

41 Guillaume Dasquié and Jean Claude Brissard, *Ben Laden. La verité interdite*, Pais: Denoël, 2001.

42 Internet sites used by the Libyan Islamic Fighting Group (LIFG) were www.libyanislamicgroup.org and www.almuqatila.com. From 2003, the first has been sabotaged and the second has been blocked.

43 Moncef Djaziri, "Libye: Kadhafi, l'Islam et les islamistes", *Confluences*, no. 12, 1994.

44 The group's declaration stated its aims as follows: "To resist such oppressors as Gaddafi has become one of the most pressing duties after belief in God itself.... The overthrow of this apostate regime and the rescue of Libya's Muslim people from this oppression can not be accomplished without injury, pain, sacrifice and the expenditure of funds. The LIFG appeals to all Muslims to take their place in this battle alongside the mujahidin and against the tyrant oppressors. The LIFG swear before God to pursue the way of Jihad until oppressin ends." Quoted by François Burgat in "Libye: chronique intérieure", *Annuaire de l'Afrique du Nord*, vol. 34, 1995, p. 607.

45 André Martel, *La Libye 1835-1990, essai de géopolitique historique*, Paris: PUF, 1991.

46 Muammar Qaddafi, *As-sijl al-qawmi bayanat wa-l ahadith al aqid Mu'ammar al-Qadhafi (Recueil des discours, 1973)*, Tripoli: World Centre for Green Book Studies. See also, Moncef Djaziri, *Etat et société en Libye*, Paris: L'Harmattan, 1996.

47 See Moncef Djaziri, *Etat et société en Libye, op. cit.*, p. 85.

48 George Joffé, "Qadhafi's Islam in Local Historical Perspective", in Dirk Vandewalle (ed.) *Qadhafi's Libya, 1969-1994*, New York: St. Martin's Press, 1995.

49 Lisa Anderson, "Qaddafi's Islam", in *Voices of Resurgent Islam*, John Esposito (ed.) Oxford University Press, 1983; and Hervé Bleuchot, "L'Islam de M. el-Qaddhafi" in *Islam et politique au Maghred*, Ernest Gellner and Jean-Claude Vatin (eds), Paris: CNRS, 1981.

50 LIFG spokesperson. www.fas.org/irp/world/para/docs/IN-LIBYA.htm: This article was published in the 15th issue of *Nida'ul Islam* magazine (http://www.islam.org.au), October - November 1996.

51 *Nid'ul Islam*, October-November 1996.

52 LIFG spokesperson. www.fas.org/irp/world/para/docs/IN-LIBYA.htm: This article was published in the 15th issue of *Nida'ul Islam* magazine (http://www.islam.org.au), October - November 1996.

53 On 21 October 1996 the spokesman of the LIFG, Abu Bakr al-Sharif, stated in an interview with the newspaper al-Hayat that the regime's strategy "sometimes obstructed military operations".

54 Luis Martinez, *La guerre civile en Algérie*, Paris: Karthala, 2000, English translation: *The Algerian Civil War*, Hurst, 2002.

55 On 22 July 1996, a communiqué from the Libyan Movement for Change and Reform condemned the regime's suppression in that month of the mutiny at Bou Salem in Tripoli, which was said to have claimed hundreds of victims. *El Hayat*, 28 July 1996.

56 According to Eric Gobe's account, from an opposition spokesman in Cairo, "the anger of the Ittihad supporters broke out when the referee, under pressure from

Saadi, gave a crucial goal to al-Ahli. His bodyguards fired at them, killing four people on the spot.... According to diplomatic sources, shots fired in the air killed between eight and 25 people." *Annuaire de l'Afrique du Nord*, no. 35, 1996, p. 507.

57 Evans Pritchard describes the functions of a "zawiya": "Sanusiya lodges served many purposes besides catering for religious needs. They were schools, caravanserai, commercial centres, social centres, forts, courts of law, banks, besides being channels through which ran a generous stream of God's blessing. They were centres of culture and security in a wild country and amid a fierce people and they were stable points in a country where all else constantly on the move.... But the chief benefits the lodges conferred on the Bedouin were ... that they and their children might learn from scholarly and pious men the faith and precepts of Islam, that they might have the opportunity to worship in a mosque, and that by charity to their lodges they might earn recompense hereafter." E. E. Evans-Pritchard, *The Sanusi of Cyrenaica*. Oxford, 1949, p. 80.

58 On the Sanusiya, see Jean Louis Triaud, *La légende noire de la Sanûsiyya: une confrérie musulmane saharienne sous le regard français: 1840-1930*, Paris: Maison des Sciences de l'Homme, 1995, 2 volumes.

59 Enzo Santarelli, Giorgio Rochat, Romain Rainero, Luigi Goglia, *Omar al Mukhtar: the Italian Reconquest of Libya*, London: DARF Publishers, 1986.

60 Majid Khadduri, *Modern Libya: A Study in Political Development*, Baltimore: Johns Hopkins Press, 1963.

61 Hervé Bleuchot, *Chroniques et documents libyens (1969-1980)*, Paris: CNRS, 1983.

62 René Lemarchand (ed.) *The Green and the Black: Qadhafi's Policies in Africa*, Bloomington: Indiana University Press, 1988.

63 The Libyan army was structured around a General Defence Committee which, together with the General Secretariat, supervised the Chief of Staff. The Chief of Staff was drawn from one of the three wings of the army: aviation and civil defence (5000 men), local popular defence, and the Popular Guard (40,000 men, including 25,000 conscripts).

64 Mansour el Kikhia, *Libya's Qaddafi. The Politics of Contradiction*, Gainesville, University of Florida Press, 1997.

65 Moncef Ouannes, "Chronique Politique – Libye", *Annuaire de l'Afrique du Nord*, Volume 37, 1998, p. 173.

66 Moncef Ouannes, op. cit., p. 174.

67 Moncef Ouannes, op. cit., p. 174.

68 Lisa Anderson, *The State and Social Transformation in Tunisia and Libya, 1830-1980*, Princeton University Press, 1987.

69 Dirk Vandewalle, "The Failure of Liberalization in the Jamahiriyya" in Dirk Vandewalle (ed.), *Qadhafi's Libya, 1969-1994*, New York: St. Martin's Press, 1995.

70 The emergence of a black market "amounting to up to 20 per cent of currency transactions, at a rate ten times the official rate", created the conditions for a prosperous unofficial economy under the sanctions. Mary-Jane Deeb, "Political and Economic Developments in Libya in the 1990s" in Yahuya H. Zoubir (ed.) *North Africa in Transi-*

tion: *State, Society and Economic Transformation in the 1990s*, University Press of Florida, 1999.

[71]   For an account of Tripoli, see Nora Lafi, *Une ville du Maghreb entre ancien régime et réformes ottomanes. Genèse des institutions à Tripoli de Barbarie (1795-1911)*, Paris: l'Harmattan, 2002.

[72]   Moncef Ouannes, "Islamistes en Libye: itinéraires idéologiques et confrontations avec le pouvoir", *Cahiers du Ceres*, no. 6., p. 261.

[73]   The artificial Great River is a scheme to direct the water of the aquifers in the Kufra-Tazebo-Sarir region to the coastal towns, at a total cost of 25 billion dollars. The first section, which serves Cyrenaica and the Gulf of Sirte, and which came into operation 1990/91, carries two million cubic metres of water per day. over a distance of 900 kilometres. The second phase of the project is intended to bring drinking water to Tripoli and its surroundings.

3. GADDAFI: HIS POWER AND POSITION

[1]   Gaddafi was born in 1942, in the neighbourhood of Sirte.

[2]   *Kadhafi: je suis un opposant à l'échelle mondiale*, [interviews with Gaddafi] Paris: Pierre-Marcel Favre, 1984.

[3]   In the words of Lisa Anderson: "Tribal imperatives were interpreted in different terms under the monarchy, which emphasized the cohesion and exclusiveness of kinship, and the revolutionary regime, which also embraced the more general principles of egalitarian participation and abhorrence of economic specialization; but both regimes turned to the idiom and reality of the tribe to win support and maintain authority." "Tribes and State: Libyan Anomalies", in *Tribes and State Formation in the Middle East*, Philip S. Khoury and Joseph Kostiner (eds) London: I.B.Tauris, 1991, p. 228.

[4]   Hervé Bleuchot, *Chroniques et Documents libyens (1969-1980)*, Paris: CNRS, 1983, p. 47.

[5]   Moammar El Qadhafi, *Le Livre Vert*, Centre Mondial d'Etudes et de recherches sur le Livre Vert, Tripoli, 3rd edition, 1999.

[6]   "The solution of the problem of democracy", *The Green Book*, chapter on "Parties", p. 11. See Abdul Fattah Chehadeh, *Démocratie. Entre al Troisième Théorie Universelle et les Conceptions Contemporaines*, Tripoli, Centre Mondial du Livre Vert, p. 11.

[7]   "La solution du problème économique", *Le Livre Vert*, op. cit. p. 41

[8]   Rémy Leveau, "Le système politique" in *La Libye nouvelle. Rupture et continuité*, Paris: CNRS, 1975, p. 85

[9]   The original members of the RCC were: Abdessalam Jallud; Mukhtar Abdallah al-Qarawi; Bashir Seghir Hawadi; Abdel Moneim el-Tahir Huni; Mustafa el-Kharrubi; Khuweidi al-Hamdi; Mohammed Najm; Awad Ali Hamza; Abu Bakr Yinus Jabr; Omar Abdallah Mesheishi; Mohammed Abu Bakr Muqayref.

10 "The Zuwara speech set the scene for the charter of the popular revolution: the suppression of current laws; the elimination of all those 'sick' individuals who opposed the progress of the revolution; complete freedom for the popular masses, who should bear arms; revolution of the administration. All useless officials were to be dismissed, and a cultural revolution should be set in motion. All alien theories contrary to Islam and to the objectives of 1 September were to be eliminated." Hervé Bleuchot, "Chroniques et documents libyens", *Annuaire de l'Afrique du Nord*, Vol. 22, 1983, p. 56.

11 Hanspetter Mattes, "The Rise and Fall of the Revolutionary Committees" in *Qadhafi's Libya, 1969-1994* (ed.) Dirk Vandewalle, New York: St. Martin's Press, 1995.

12 Eva Bellin, "The Robustness of Authoritarianism in the Middle East", *Comparative Politics*, vol. 36, no. 2, January 2004.

13 Abdellah Bilal, *the Jamahiriyya and the Victory of the Age of the Masses*, Tripoli: Green Book Center.

14 David Blundy and Andrew Lycett, *Qaddafi and the Libya Revolution*, Boston: Brown and Company, 1987, and Hanspetter Mattes, op. cit.

15 A rentier State is defined by Hazem Beblawi as a State which derives a substantial part of its income from abroad, in the form of "rent". See, Hazem Beblawi and Luciani Giacomo. *The Rentier State*. London: Croom Helm, 1987. A distributive State is one whose expenditure represents a major part of the national income. See Yasuyuki Matsunaga, "L'état rentier est-il réfractaire à la démocratie?" *Critique Internationale*, no. 8, July 2000.

16 François Burgat and André Laronde, *La Libye*, Paris: Que sais-je?, 1996.

17 Dirk Vandewalle, *Libya Since Independence: Oil and State-Building*, Ithaca: Cornell University Press, 1998.

18 The development plan of 1973-1975 enabled the construction of 115,552 housing units, 21 hospitals, 39 dental clinics, 61 maternity units and 102 health centres. Omar El Fathaly and Monte Palmer, *Political Dvelopment and Social Change in Libya*, Lexington: Lexington Books, 1980, p. 189.

19 Hanspetter Mattes puts it as follows: "Up until the present, the revolutionary leadership's deployment of the security organisations to protect the revolution has been so efficient that any attempts to depose the regime or to change the political system by oppositional military or political groups had been doomed to failure." See: "The Libyan Case" (article presented to workshop on "Challenges of security sector governance in the Middle East", Geneva, 12-13 July 2004.

20 Claude Monnier, "Les forces armées libyennes ou le peuple en armes", *Revue de défense nationale*, November 1984.

21 The Libyan army was established in 1951 on the basis of the "Libyan Arab Force". At the time, the army was no less than 5000 strong, against 11,000 in the police, including many former members of the Sanusi Legion. The police were better equipped, and — together with the Cyrenaica Defence Force — constituted an élite corps. The Royal Guard had been recruited in Kufra.

22 Intelligence Report, 2 September 1993, www.globalsecurity.org.

23 Interestingly, Gaddafi saw the institution of the Revolutionary Committees as similar to the nervous system in the body. "It will not be a party or a vanguard. Nor will it be any of the institutions which dominate the people. It will be something similar to the nerves in the human body. The body of man is constituted in such an integral way that it carries out its own function, But it cannot move without a nerve moving each part of it. Like the hand for example, which is an integral part but cannot move unless a nerve moves it." Quoted by Hasnawi, op. cit.

24 Ammunition stores, for example, were under the control of officials of the security services.

25 However, Libya has substantial armaments at its disposal. "Libya's land forces have a total of 2020 tanks, 1130 Armoured Infantry Fighting Vehicles, 990 Armoured Personnel Carriers, 444 self-propelled artillery pieces, 647 towed artillery pieces, and 830 Multiple Rocket Launchers. Its air forces consist of 400 combat aircraft and 41 attack helicopters. Its naval forces have one submarine, 2 major surface ships, 8 missile patrol craft, 2 mine warfare ships and 3 amphibious ships. These totals are impressive for a relatively small country, but much of this force is in storage or non-operational, combat readiness and modernisation rates are very poor." *The Military Balance*, London: International Institute of Strategic Studies, 2004.

26 *Maghreb Confidential*, no. 595, 20 March 2003.

27 "Popular violence has remained at a low level in Libya. No general demonstration took place in the entire period from 1971 to 1985, and there have been only eight small-scale demonstrations and one strike." Muhammad Safi al-Din, "La violence politique en Jamahiriyya arabe Libyenne", in P. Dupret (ed), *Phénomène de la violence politique*, Cairo: Dossiers du Cedej, 1994, p. 177.

28 Kiren Aziz Chaudhry, "Economic Liberalization and the Lineages of the Rentier State", *Comparative Politics*, No. 27 October, 1994.

29 In the Zuwara speech of 16 April 1973, Gaddafi included in his five points "the elimination of all bad elements opposed to the progress of the revolution". See Hervé Bleuchot, "Chroniques et documents Libyens, 1969-1980", Paris: CNRS, 1983, p. 56.

30 For a critique of the theory of the "Rentier State", see Yasuyuki Matsunaga, "L'état rentier est-il réfractaire à la démocratie", *Critique Internationale*, no.8, July 2000.

31 John Davis, *Libyan Politics: Tribe and Revolution*, London: I.B.Tauris, 1987.

32 "The Sanusi success was rooted in biuilding on and adapting to this tribal social organisation", Ali Abdullah Ahmida, *The Making of Modern Libya*, Albany: State University of New York Press, 1994, p. 81.

33 André Martel, *La Libye, 1835-1990. Essai de géographie historique*, Paris: PUF, 1991.

34 J. C. Hurewitz, *Middle East Politics: the military dimension*, New York: Octagon Books, 1974, p. 233.

35 *The Green Book*, Volume 1", Tripoli: World Centre for Study and Research on the Green Book, p. 274.

36 Significant tribal figures include Colonel Ahmad Gaddaf al-Dam, military commander of Cyrenaica, and General Sayyid Muhammad Gaddaf al-Dam, the governor of the Sirte region.

37 Mansour El Kikhia, op. cit., p. 90.

38 www.gaddaficharity.org.

39 "I have decided to love you, Aisha and to ask you directly and formally to marry me, as you are responsible for yourself according to the Third Universal Theory. I am telling you frankly, I am prepared to do anything to make you my wife.... I will even go before the tribunals of history and swear that your father, the revolutionary leader, did not oppose the decision to halt the supply of oil to the western world in 1973, but that this it was only a cruel rumour,... I shall help you write a new book, which I suggest you call the Blonde Book, which shall be the Green Book for the 21st century. We can also change the Libyan flag from Green to Blonde. But, Aisha, I must insist there have to be some limits. Can it be that the future leader of the revolution will wear jeans and American dress?" Al-Majallah, 19 November, 2000.

40 The freeing of 107 political prisoners in August 2001 was a demonstration that Libya wanted to shed the image of an authoritarian regime.

41 However, a clandestine journal "La'" — which means "No" in Arabic — made its appearance during the sanctions period, denouncing the practices of the regime.

42 "Musa Kusa is, according to the Libyan exiled opposition, also one of Qaddafi's relatives. After studying in the United States (his master's thesis was entitled "The political leader and his social background: Muammar Qaddafi, the Libyan leader, Michigan State University, 1978), Musa Kusa became Head of the Libyan People's Bureau in London. From the mid-1980 to 1982 he was active in the so-called al Mathaba al Alamiya as a leading figure. The Mathaba was disbanded as an independent organisation in October 1992 and continues as External Security within the Jamahiriya Security Organisation." Hanspetter Mattes, "Challenges to Security Sector Governance in the Middle East", op.cit. p. 14.

43 Abdul Salem Zadmeh was a member of Gaddafi's close circle and was the Mayor of Tripoli. He died in July 1998.

44 Africa Confidential, 8 March 1991.

45 According to a report in the journal Arabies: "At the end of 2002, more than 130 Libyan projects were completed or in the course of completion in 26 of the 46 sub-Saharan countries." Libyan investment in Africa reached 4 billion dollars, "ten times the total of investments and gifts between 1970 and 1977". Arabies, February 2003, p. 21.

46 On 22 October 2002, the Jana news agency officially confirmed Libya's decision to withdraw from the Arab League. In October 2003, Gaddafi made a speech in the town of Sebha, in which he said: "The Arabs are being crushed today in Palestine and Iraq. Everything Libya has endued in the past is the result of our support for the Arabs. In spite of our sacrifices, they allied themselves with the United States and with Zionism. There is no further hope for them." Quoted in Jeune Afrique/L'intelligent, no. 2232, 19-25 October 2003.

47 L'Autre Afrique, 18-25 March 1998.

48   René Otayek, *La politique africaine de la Libye*, Paris: Karthala, 1986.
49   Interview with Gaddafi, *L'Autre Afrique*, 18-245 March 1998.
50   *Le Figaro*, August 20 1999.
51   The Union Of Investments in Africa, in its Chapter 3, provided for "The promotion of investment in Africa and efforts towards the creation of an African common market in which goods and commodities of African origin will be freely exchanged; striving for the unification of the economy of Africa and the realisation of monetary union and the African common market; working towards the unification of customs tariffs between African States." See: Statutes of the Union for Investment in Africa, *Le rêve d'Afrique*, pamphlet published in Tripoli.
52   *La Revue Parlementaire*, June 2005, p. 11.
53   Gaddafi's speech in July 2001 at the establishment of the African Union, *Géopolitique africaine*, no.4, November 2001.
54   Paolo Pezzino, "La mafia, Etat et société dans la Sicile contemporaine", *Politix*, no, 49, 2000, p. 17

4. IS THE JAMAHIRIYA REFORMABLE?

1   Christopher Boucek, "Libya's Return to the Fold", *Foreign Policy in Focus*, April 2004.
2   H. Albrecht and O. Schlumberger, "Waiting for Godot: Regime Change without Democratization in the Middle East", *International Political Science Review*, vol. 25, no. 4, October 2004, pp. 371-392.
3   B. Hibou, "Les marges de manoeuvre d'un 'bon élève économique': la Tunisie de Ben Ali", Etudes du CERI, no. 60, 1999; B. Hibou "Economie politique du discours de la Banque mondiale en Afrique sub-saharienne: du catéchisme économique au fait (et méfait) missionaire", Etudes du CERI, no. 39, 1998.
4   See, for example, Shukri Ghanem, *The Pricing of Libyan Crude Oil*, La Valette: Adams Pubishing, 1975; *The Economy of Libya before the Oil Era* [in Arabic], Tripoli, n.d.
5   According to the British consultants Robertson Research International Ltd., Libya is a prime target for investment in the petroleum industry. Only 25 per cent of the oil and gas reserves, estimated at 40 billion barrels, are being exploited. Information from interview with Tarek Hassan, director of planning at the Libyan NOC, *New York Times*, 23 July 2004.
6   *Arab Oil and Gas Directory*, Paris: Arab Petroleum research Center, 2000.
7   *Middle East Economic Digest*, 18 August 2000.
8   Oksana Antonenko explains: "Between 1970 and 1991, Russia supplied 19 billion dollars of military equipment to the Libyan armed forces. More than 90 per cent of Libyan military equipment is Soviet and Russian made. ... After sanctions were lifted in 1999, Russia sought to renew its arms sales including platforms, spare parts, and modernization contracts for Libyan equipment. However, Russia's hopes on major contracts for the Libyan armed forces so far remain unfulfilled due to unsettled debts

- the largest part being 3 billion dollars for contracts unfulfilled due to sanctions. ... In August 2000, the Russian vice-premier in charge of the military-industrial structure, Ilya Klebanov, announced that Russia's expectations towards military-technical cooperation with Libya so far have not been realised because 'Tripoli has not taken the political decision to develop large scale military cooperation with Russia'. ... It appears likely that in case of complete removal of political sanctions towards Libya from European States, the Libyan government, which possesses significant financial resources for modernization of its armed forces, is likely to look to the West for major new import contracts". *Middle East Review of International Affairs*, vol. 5, no. 1, March 2001, p. 8.

9   On 5 February 2005, Michèle Alliot-Marie, France's Defence Minister, went to Tripoli to sign what was described as a "framework agreement", which provided for "the opportunity for French participation in the renewal and modernisation of Libya's military equipment." *La Revue Parlementaire*, June 2005, p. 35.

10   "It is a well known fact that one of the EU member states – and therefore all member states because of the open borders – is having considerable problems with illegal immigrants coming from Libya. The Ministers agreed today that cooperation with Libya on the topic of migration has become a pressing matter." Declaration of Luxembourg, General Affairs and External Relations Council, European Union Foreign Ministers. www.eu2004.nl/default.asp.

11   Text of Colonel Gaddafi's speech unofficially communictaed to the author.

12   Michael L. Ross, "The Political Economy of the Resource Curse", *World Politics*, 51, January 1999.

13   "A Brief Information Guide to Doing Business in Libya", www.exportmichigan. com.

14   *Jeune Afrique*, 22-28 June, p. 72.

15   International Anti-Corruption Conference, Durban, 10 October 1999. ww1.transparency.org/iacc/9th_iacc/ papers/day1/ws5/dnld/d1ws5_amaabbar.pdf.

16   *Maghreb Confientiel*, no.622, 30 October 2003. In relation to funds held by oil states, Thierry Coville has written as follows. "Some years ago it was supposed that the creation of stabilisation oil funds was a solution. The idea was to place excess oil income – in other words oil income in excess of what had been budgeted for – in a fund which would be used to sustain the economy at times when oil prices fall. However, experience shows that such funds are not a solution when the principles of transparency and rigour are not applied to budgetary policy. On the contrary, such funds, in the present state of development of institutions in the Middle East, only serve to exacerbate patronage and corruption." Thierry Coville, "Des économies du Moyen-Orient marquées par la malédiction de la rente pétrolière", www.strategicsinternational.com.

17   www.nfsl-libya.com.

18   *Arabies*, Febvruary 2003, p. 21.

19   Michel Seurat, *L'État de Barbarie*, Paris: Seuil, 1977, p. 131.

20   Under the provisions of law number 1 of 1993, on privatisation.

21 IMF, Public Information Notice (PIN) No. 03/125, October 23, 2003, Consultation with the Socialist People's Libyan Jamahiriya, www.imf.org/external.

22 Zidan Mohammed, "Libye: la fin des illusions", *La Lettre du CERMAM*, no, 9. December 2005.

23 For example, between 2003 and 2008, the government envisages the transfer of 360 units of production enterprises out of the public sector and into private ownership. *El Fajr el-Jadid*, 18 December 2003.

24 Interview eith Ammar Eltief in *Marchés Tropicaux*, 2 June 2000.

25 Decree number 9 of 9 September 1999.

26 An article in the New York Times provides an illustration of these concerns: "Another problem is corruption..... The country still seems ill-equipped to deal with the influx of foreigners. Recently, a high-level representative from the World Bank, Yukiro Omura, who was scheduled to deliver a speech here, was denied entry at the airport because of problems with her visa.... As a result, foreign investors remain cautious". *New York Times*, 2 January 2005.

27 Yahuya Zoubir, "Libya in US Foreign Policy: from rogue state to good fellow?", *Third World Quarterly*, vol. 23, no. 1, p. 44.

28 *Maghreb Confidentiel*, no. 551, 4 April 2002.

29 Libya Country Analysis Brief, January 2004, www.eia.doe.gov.

30 www.noclibya.com

31 Judith Gurney, *Libya: the Political Economy of Energy*, Oxford University Press, 1996.

32 www.noclibya.com

33 Libya Country Analysis Brief, February 2005, www.eia.doe.gov

34 Clement Moore Henry, [Clement Henry Moore] "Algeria's Agonies: Oil Rent Effects in a Bunker State". The Journal of North African Studies, vol.9, no.2, 2004.

35 *Maghreb Confidentiel*, no. 641, 18 March 2004.

36 *Maghreb Confidentiel*, no. 551, 4 April 2004.

37 "Oil giant Exxon returns to Libya", BBC, news.bbc.co.uk, 6 December 2005; *Petroleum Economist*, June 2005.

38 John Anthony Allan, *Libya: the Experience of Oil*, Boulder: Westview Press, 1981.

39 Economist Intelligence Unit, "Libya Country Report", 4th quarter 1998, p. 21

40 Libya Country Analysis Brief, February 2005, www.eia.doe.gov

41 George Joffé, "La Libye et l'Europe", *Maghreb-Machrek*, no. 170, October-December 2000.

42 OPEC , Annual Statistical Bulletin, 2003.

43 *Arab Oil and Gas Directory*, Paris: Arab Petroleum Research Center, 2000, p. 247-248.

44 D Cortright and G.A,Lopez, *The Sanctions Decade: assessing the UN in the 1990s*, Boulder: Westview, 2000.

45 W.A.Otman and M.A.G.Bunter, "The Libyan Petroleum Industry in the Twenty First Century", *Alexander's Oil and Gas Connections*, May 2005.

46 Jean-Jacques Regnier and Larbi Talha, "Les problèmes de développement économique", *La Libye Nouvelle*, Paris: CNRS, 1975.

47   See Daryl Champion, *The Paradoxical Kingdom, Saudi Arabia and the Momentum of Reform*, London: Hurst, 2003.

48   Ali Aissaoui, *Algeria: the Political Economy of Oil and Gas*, Oxford University Press, 2001, p. 312.

49   Frank.C. Waddams, *The Libyan Oil Industry*, London: Croom Helm, 1980, p. 338.

50   *Arab Oil and Gas Directory*, Paris: Arab Petroleum research Center, 2000.

51   Law number 24 of 5 March 1970 replaced LIPETCO (the Libyan General Petroleum Corporation) by the National Oil Corporation. Law 69 of 4 July 1970 gave the NOC monopoly control over oil imports and exports.

52   Shukri Ghanem, *The Pricing of Libyan Crude Oil*, La Vallette: Adams Publishing, 1975.

53   Judith Gurney, *Libya the Political Economy of Energy*, Oxford University Press, 1996.

54   Jean Jacques Regnier and Larbi Talha, "Les problèmes de développement économique", dans *La Libye Nouvelle*, Paris: CNRS, 1975, p. 221.

55   Nevertheless, Libya currently operates three refineries (at Ras Lanuf, Zawiya and Sarir) with a total capacity of 349 thousand bpd, as well as three refineries in Europe (Cremonia, Holborn and Collombey) with a capacity of 300,000 bpd. Libya has nine ports (Zuwara, Tripoli, Al-Khums, Misurata, Sirte, Brega, Benghazi, Derna, Tobruk) and a similar number of civil airports. Libya also has a substantial road system with 25 thousand kilometres of roads. The plan to build 3170 kilometres of railways is once more on the table. The Great Underground River project, which aims to pump six million cubic metres from the water table under the Sahara to the coast, is at phase 3 of five planned stages. Investment to date total 25 billion dollars. See: "La Libye: pourquoi pas?", *Marchés Tropicaux*, 2 June 2000.

56   Paul Balta, *Le Grand Maghreb: des indépendances à l'an 2000*, La Découverte, 2000.

57   Gérard Destanne de Bernis, "La Libye et l'Algérie: stratégies de développement comparées", *Annuaire de l'Afrique du Nord*, Volume X, 1971, pp. 267-296.

58   See "Algeria", in *Arab Oil and Gas Directory*, 2000.

59   In the field of gas, Agip in collaboration with the NOC was most involved in the West Libya Gas Project. In 1999, an agreement signed by the NOC and Agip North Africa provide for an investment of 5.5 billion dollars. The project was to export Libyan gas to Italy by way of Sicily. See: *Matahab.net/news*.

60   On 1985, Agip discovered large gas resources in Libya, which it proposed to link to the Transmed Pipleline. Agip opened talks with Algeria, Libya and Tunisia on joint exploitation. The exploitation of Libya's El-Wafa oilfield, discovered in 1981, was an example of the potentialities of joint operation. A pipeline had to be constructed to the terminals before it could go into production. One possible solution would have been to transfer its output to the Alrar field in Algeria. This site, built in 1985 by the Soviets, was linked directly by pipeline to Hassi R'Mel. In the event, Total, Agip, Repsol and Lasmo all took positions in El-Wafa in the prospect that Algerian-Libya cooperation could result in joint production. See Judith Gurney, *Libya the Political Economy of Energy*, Oxford University Press, 1996.

61   Euromed Report 23 May 2003. Europa.eu.int/comm/exteranlrelations/eurome/
     publication.htm.
62   Martin Sicker, *The Making of a Pariah State: the Adventurist Politics of Muammar Qaddafi*,
     New York: Praeger, 1987, p. 140.

CONCLUSION — AFTER GADDAFI?

1   Coping with Libya's "business culture" demands patience, understanding and a sense
     of humour. At the conference held by the CFCE (Centre français du commerce ex-
     térieur) on 26 June 2003, on how to do business in Libya, all the participants drew
     attention to Libyan idiosyncrasies. One reported that "you need a lot of understand-
     ing and a sense of humour to operate in the country, as the decision making processes
     are very complicated. Never change your point of contact and always keep promises.
     Everybody in Libya takes money. It is not a question of time." Commercial relations
     are based on confidence and not just on interest and profitability. In addition, the
     lack of transparency and unpredictability of the system gives investors the impres-
     sion, according to Coface [the French organisation which insures trade risks], that the
     system operates "without knowing what is in the 5-year plans". In such a situation,
     intermediaries are indispensable: they make contacts, smooth relationships, and give
     credibility to commitments. Nonetheless, the bases on which Libya negotiates are
     dictated by current foreign policy, military and political considerations. See: Magh-
     reb Confidentiel (Archives), www.africaintelligence.fr/mc-/archives.
2   Jana News Agency, 7 July 2004.
3   Isabelle Saint-Saëns, "Des camps en Europe aux camps de l'Europe", *Multitudes*, 19,
     Winter 2004.
4   The Libyan League for Human Rights, "A judiciary without justice", 15 January
     2005. Published by allibyah@yahoo.com, quoted in www.euromedrights.net.
5   "A Vision of Libya's Future" www.mees.com/postedarticles/ politics/ArabPress-
     Review.

LIBYA CHRONOLOGY

1911: Italy invades Libya

1922-1931: Resistance to the Italian occupation

1942: A military administration is set up after the defeat of the Italian troops

1945: Great Britain occupies Tripolitania and Cyrenaica; France occupies the Fezzan

24 December 1951: Libya, under King Idris al-Sanussi, proclaims its independence from the United Kingdom.

1959: Oil reserves discovered

1 September 1969: M. Gaddafi leads a *coup d'état* with a group of Free Officers

1977: Proclamation of the Jamahiryya

24 March 1986: Armed confrontation between American and Libyan forces in the Gulf of Sirte

15 April 1986: American air raids over Tripoli and Benghazi

1987: Ceasefire signed with Chad

21 December 1988: Pan Am flight 103 explodes over Lockerbie, Scotland: 270 dead

19 September 1989: A UTA DC10 aircraft explodes over the Tenere Desert in Niger, 170 dead

15 April 1992: The UN Security Council imposes an air and military embargo

October 1993: Financial assets frozen and embargo on crude oil equipment

1996: clashes with Islamist groups

1998: Sahara & Sahel summit in Tripoli

179

5 April 1999: Sanctions lifted

March 2001: African Union founded

June 2003: Shukri Ghanem becomes Prime Minister

13 August 2003: an agreement is reached to pay 2.7 billion dollars to indemnify British and American families of victims of the Lockerbie bombing

12 September 2003: The UN Security Council passes Resolution 1506 lifting all sanctions

19 December 2003: Libya abandons its weapons of mass destruction programme

9 January 2004: Libya promises to pay 170 million dollars to the families of the victims of the bombing of UTA's DC10

27 April 2004: Gaddafi makes an official trip to Brussels

21 September 2004: End of the U.S. trade embargo on Libya

11 October 2004: European ban lifted on arms sales to Tripoli

January 2005: People's Courts abolished

17-20 April 2005: Official visit by the President of the European Parliament Subcommittee on Human Rights

23 April 2005: HRW Mission to Libya

17 February 2006: Demonstration in Benghazi in front of the Italian Consulate, 11 dead, 60 wounded

3 March 2006: Al Baghdadi Ali Mahmoudi replaces Shukri Ghanem as Prime Minister

21 August 2006: Seif al Islam calls for the end of the Revolutionary era and for a transformation of the Revolution towards a constitutional state

1 September 2006: 37th anniversary of the Revolution

INDEX

Abu Nidal Organization, 50
Ahmida, Ali Abdullah, 98, 172
Al Kikhia, Mansour, 59
Al Qa'ida, 58
Allan, John Anthony, 176
Anderson, Lisa, 168, 169, 170
Annan, Kofi, 8

Bayart, Jean-François, 165
Beblawi, Hazem, 159, 171
Bellin,Eva, 159, 171
Blair, Tony, 47, 140, 155
Bleuchot, Hervé, 24, 89, 162, 169, 170, 171, 172
Boubakri,Hassan, 164
Bouteflika, Abdelaziz, 57
Boutros-Ghali, Boutros, 13
Bruce, St John Ronald, 166, 167
Bruguière, Jean-Louis, 9
Brumberg, Daniel, 159
Burgat, François, 168, 171
Bush, George, W, 43, 45, 49, 51, 138

Camau, Michel, 159
Collins, Stephen, D, 52
Davis, John, 98, 172
Deeb, Mary-Jane, 170

Destanne De Bernis, Gérard, 147, 177
Djaziri, Moncef, 161, 168

El Hami, Mohamed, 64
El Libi, Anas, 49, 61

Fhima, Lamen Khalifa, 49

Gaddafi, Seif al Islam, 7, 12, 83, 101, 102, 103, 104, 107, 114, 140, 153, 156, 157
Gurney, Judith, 176, 177
General People's Congress, 17, 19, 20, 22
Ghariany, Bashir, 22, 162
Ghanem Shukri, 101, 103, 106, 118, 127, 131, 134, 135, 139, 156, 174
Gobe, Eric, 168, 169
Grégoire, Emmanuel, 33, 165

Hibou,Béatrice, 165, 174
Hussein, Saddam, 5, 6, 7, 11, 45, 46, 58, 134, 154

Islamic Jihad, 59
Islamic Martyrs' Movement, 64

Jalloud, Abdessalam, 93, 97, 99
Joffé, George, 168

Khaduri, Majid, 169
King Idris, 4, 18, 31, 67, 76, 85, 86, 87, 88, 98, 144, 158
Kusa, Musa, 49, 52, 56, 101, 103, 105, 107, 165, 173

Lafi, Nora, 170
LAFICO (Libyan Arab Foreign Investment Company), 16, 116
Lemarchand, René, 167, 169
Leveau, Rémy, 4, 88, 160, 170
Libyan Arab African Investment Company (LAAICO), 127
Libyan Islamic Fighting Group (LIFG), 43, 49, 59, 61, 62, 63, 64, 68, 69, 70
Libyan Movement for Change and Reform (LMCR), 58, 65
Libyan National Alliance (LNA), 59
Libyan Patriotic Army, 58
Lynn, Karl Terry, 160

Maghrahi, Abdel Basset Ali, 49
Martel, André, 168, 172
Mathaba International, 52, 105, 107
Mattes, Hanspetter, 171, 173
Meshishi, Omar el, 24
Muslim Brotherhood, 59, 156

National Front for Salvation of Libya (NSFL), 58,65, 127

Neumann, Ronald E, 50
Otayek, René, 163, 174
Ouannes, Moncef, 164, 169, 170

Prodi, Romano, 111, 112
Purification Committees, 38, 40, 41, 63, 77, 78

Reagan, Ronald, 45, 53, 138, 142
Revolutionary Command Council, 24
Revolutionary Committees, 23, 29, 37, 38, 39, 49, 60, 64, 66, 67, 70, 74, 77, 80, 89, 90, 92, 93, 97, 100, 129
Rice, Condoleezza, 44
Ross, Michael, L, 124, 160, 175

Safi al-Din, Muhammad, 172
Saleh, Abdelrahim, 46
Seurat, Michel, 128
Sha'biyat, 20,22,23
Society for the Call to Islam, 68

Takfir wa-l Hijra, 59
Triki, Ali, 25, 96
Terrorist State, 7,8,56
Triaud, Jean Louis, 169

Vandewalle, Dirk, 37, 161, 162, 169, 171

Zoubir, Yahuya, 49, 159, 166, 170, 176